What There is to Love About a Man

Sourcebooks, Inc.®
Naperville, IL

by Rachel Snyder

Published by Sourcebooks, Inc.
P.O. Box 372
Naperville, IL 60566
630-961-3900
Fax: 630-961-2168

Snyder, Rachel.
      What there is to love about a man / Rachel Snyder.
            p.   cm.
      ISBN 1-57071-463-0
      1. Men.   2. Masculinity.   I. Title.
      HQ1090.S655   1999
      305.31—dc21   99-31058
                                                     CIP

            Printed and bound in the United States of America
                  10   9   8   7   6   5   4   3   2   1

Table of Contents

table of contents

by DAVID OUELLET

TRAFFIC LIGHTS **Solution: 5 letters**

N	H	T	I	S	N	A	R	T	S	E	L	B	A	C	R	C	Y	B	S
S	E	L	R	E	D	S	I	H	G	H	S	U	R	O	O	T	U	P	P
T	E	E	R	T	S	M	S	A	N	K	C	U	T	S	E	L	O	R	D
S	D	N	R	A	E	A	S	R	S	C	L	C	L	F	B	T	O	E	B
D	L	S	I	G	L	S	E	C	I	E	E	P	A	U	S	E	Z	R	E
E	Y	A	N	F	E	V	Y	R	S	T	I	S	V	T	C	I	E	D	T
D	N	A	M	M	O	C	T	R	E	E	Y	R	R	D	R	K	I	A	A
O	H	M	L	G	L	C	E	D	T	A	T	A	E	E	Y	U	Y	L	R
C	G	B	O	E	E	A	A	E	R	N	T	A	T	S	G	R	A	D	E
N	U	E	W	L	D	N	H	D	T	S	E	U	N	S	T	N	R	K	P
O	O	R	E	Y	G	A	L	W	N	R	P	M	I	R	G	R	A	U	O
I	R	A	R	E	N	R	L	O	S	M	U	E	I	I	E	R	E	N	H
T	H	L	R	G	I	E	I	R	O	K	E	C	S	N	B	T	O	A	T
A	T	F	I	H	S	T	H	C	N	C	C	H	K	U	U	I	L	N	K
L	E	N	D	T	S	A	F	I	N	W	A	A	R	O	T	T	I	A	Y
U	G	L	E	E	O	L	L	A	G	D	A	N	R	U	L	O	E	E	Y
C	T	H	G	I	R	B	V	T	E	H	T	I	A	T	P	E	L	S	T
R	A	N	A	N	C	D	Y	T	U	D	W	C	T	X	U	L	F	N	I
I	O	R	T	R	A	N	S	P	O	R	T	A	T	I	O	N	L	T	C
C	O	N	S	T	R	U	C	T	I	O	N	L	Y	W	O	L	L	O	F

...ea around the
...ilding uncov-
...red a blood-
...meared hammer,
...hich proved to
...e the murder
...eapon. Someone
...ad brutally blud-
...eoned Staga to
...eath for a used
...elevision set.

A blue Ply-
...outh sedan was
...arked outside
...taga's apartment. It was regis-
...red in the name of Lawrence
...eyes. While the investigation was
...king place, Reyes and an old
...iend, Juan Venegas, flagged
...own a patrol car to report that his
...lymouth had been stolen.

It took detectives only a few days
... gather evidence against Reyes.
... his home, detectives found
...taga's wallet and a pair of bloody
...ousers. Reyes' palm print was
...ted from Staga's apartment.
...ree witnesses were located who
...aced him in the area of the crime
... the time it was committed.

Police did not have much of a
...se against Venegas, who was in
...ong Beach visiting his old friend
... the holidays. More evidence
...as required before Venegas could
... taken into custody. This was
...on forthcoming. A witness, who
...aimed to have seen men running
...om the apartment building with
...e TV, told police that one of the
...en was dressed in the same type
... clothing worn by Venegas when
...e and Reyes flagged down a pa-
...ol officer to report Reyes' stolen

Max
HAINES
CRIME FLASHBACK

...iend. Early on Christ-
mas morning, Reyes
came back to his home
and told him his car had
been stolen. Together
they went down to the
street. When a police
car drove by, they
flagged it down and re-
ported the car stolen.

Contrary to Venegas'
claims, there was evi-
dence connecting him
to the crime. A bartend-
er testified that the two friends had
been drinking in his bar moments
before the murder took place. Fo-
rensic experts said that physical
evidence at the crime scene indi-
cated that two men had taken part
in the crime.

Both men were found guilty of
first-degree murder and sentenced
to life in prison.

The case against Venegas had
been nowhere near as strong as
that against the self-confessed kill-
er, Reyes. Many believed that Venegas had been wrongly convicted.

...ing become con...
dence at trial ha...
conviction. As a
was released fro...

Venegas insti...
against the city
and three of its ...
As part of his ac...
ed an affidavit fr...
er whose eviden...
instrumental in
The bartender r...
that at the time ...
trial he had bee...
timidated by the
vestigating offic...

ed that the evi-
t warranted a
lt, Venegas
stody.

d a civil action
ng Beach
e officers.
he present-
he bartend-
ad been so
onviction.
led
e

o

prison, he lost
the farm. In ad-
dition, despite
his vindica-
tion, he found
it impossible

Provinzano

WONDERWORD ™

HOW TO PLAY: First read the list of words, then look at the puzzle. The words are in all directions — vertically, horizontally, diagonally, backward. Circle each letter of a word found and strike it off the list. The letters are often used more than once, so do not cross them out. It is best to find the big words first. When you find all the words listed in the clues, you'll have a number of letters left over that spell the Wonderword.

CLUES

Advance	Crowded	Hill	Series
Alternates	Curb	Hurry	Shade
Amber	Cycle	Influx	Shift
Angle	Danger	Interval	Signal
Blink	Delay	Later	Slam
Brake	Detector	Left	Staged
Bright	Duty	Lens	Start
Bulb	Electric	Lower	Stay
Burnt	Entry	Lucky	Stops
Cables	Fast	Mechanical	Streak
Cars	Fines	Message	Street
Caution	Flare	Minutes	Stuck
Change	Flash	Operate	Through
Circulation	Follow	Pause	Time
City	Gates	Point	Tracks
Coded	Govern	Rays	Transit
Color	Grade	Ready	Transportation
Command	Green	Reds	Truck
Computerized	Guide	Route	Turn
Congestion	Hanging	Rules	Wait
Construction	Heed	Rush	Yellow
Crossing	Highway	Safety	

Acknowledgments

acknowledgments

Thanks to God for loving me so much and providing always, to Charlie for constantly revealing more and more things to love about a man, to Sharon for introducing me to Sourcebooks, and to my editor Deborah Werksman for being sufficiently wise and sizzling to understand and appreciate why this book matters.

What There is to Love About a Man

mystery

Certain aspects of being a man will always remain a mystery. To a woman, certainly. To certain men, perhaps. And the fact of this unknowingness is part of what we love. This unfathomable mystery draws us in, yet the door will not open. The maze beckons us, mystifies us, yet we cannot make our way through the labyrinth. Obscurity reigns supreme. It is the nature of mystery to bewilder us. To move just out of reach at the exact instant that we believe we have figured it out. Clues arouse us, even as true understanding eludes us. We may observe a man, adore a man, appreciate a man, and love a man. Our brains may even hold some comprehension of what it is to be a man. But unless we fully live the life of a man, we will never really fathom the being of a man. Who can say? It's the truth. It's inexplicable. It's a mystery.

1

Fire

Something inside a man sizzles. Red-hot coals lie aglow in his belly, waiting for the breath of inspiration that will set them aflame. This is the fire that lives in a man. These are the roots of his passion, his fervor, his fuel to create a well-tempered existence. Herein lies his tinderbox, awaiting to arouse a man to a luminous life. When his fire is tended and nourished and fed, a man can kindle a revolt of his spirit, and awaken a brilliance as bright as the sun. He need only build the proper hearth to channel this white-hot intensity into the energy of action. To build and to dance; to begin and to be. To radiate a light that shines from within and enlightens all in his orbit—and nobody needs to get burned. A man has the power to be a firebug for his very soul, but first he must find his very own matches. And then, he must play with his fire.

Jeans

Thank you, Levi Strauss, for giving us jeans! Rear-hugging, thigh-rubbing, leg-loving jeans! Standing up in the corner after a week of muck and mud, or hanging crisp and creased for a weekend of merriment and mirth, jeans fit a man everywhere a man ought to be fit. Like down in the cellar or out back of the barn. Sundays at the clinic, or Saturdays at Little League practice. Buttons and zippers and rivets, oh my! Painted-on jeans, sitting atop dusty boots or wrapped around his Harley. Loose and baggy jeans, riding perilously low when he's trying to caulk that hole under the sink. Jeans just right, when he's meeting his son's new sweetheart for noodles and getting-to-know-you. When he's sitting on a rock and staring off into a distant place. Pay attention and you can learn a lot from a man's jeans. Like what road he's been walking down—and how much dust he's kicked up along the way.

legacy

He's planting seeds now to leave something behind. His home, his business, the collection of WWII memorabilia he's gathered from flea markets and yard sales and families he's never met. He's making sure he leaves a part of himself in his children. His stories, his values, his shiny black curls, and those absolutely unforgettable eyes. Down at the plant, they'll always remember the way he cooled tempers during the strike. Over at the school, his love of learning will live forever in the minds of his students and then they'll pass it on. Anyone who ever heard him sing on a street corner will carry his melody for a lifetime. Everyone who saw the way he cared for his parents or carved masks out of marble or planted wildflowers by the roadside will remember what they saw. Let it be known for all time that he was the first to do what he did. And let us give thanks that his best will live on.

Mustache

mustache

Some men must mustache. Ever since the bright bathroom light first revealed those baby-fine hairs, they knew they would never remove them. It's not enough for them to have a tiny tickler above the lip, they need an out-and-out guffaw. A soup-strainer of impeccable style. A mustachio glorioso! Dashing and debonair like David Niven, barely there yet such precision! Bushy and brushy and bristling with brawn. *That one's so dark—has it been drawn on?* Handlebars with ends twisted and curled and greased up just right. Gold and glistening, gray and peppery, white as Santa, black as night. Many a man wishes for Wild Bill whiskers, for that caterpillar who gently warms his upper lip and never moves a hair. Nightly trimmed or scarcely scissored, pencil-thin or slipping south, a mustache hides a multitude of sins and brings that certain something to most any man's mouth.

Spontaneity

Let's go canoeing on the lake. *Now!* How about running to the bagel store? *Get up!* Want to elope and drive to Vegas? *Come on!* Put down that book, *it's time to go bowling!* Put on your shoes, *I'm taking us dancing!* TV is boring, *let's retile the bathroom!* Interest rates are dropping, *let's go buy a house!* Let's bolt up to Sundance and see a few movies! Let's get the 5:20 and sleep on the train! See you next Spring, *I'm moving to Maui!* I'm sick of my navel! *Why not get a piercing?* Got a few minutes? *Let's all shave our heads!* Hungry for brioche? *Let's go grab the Concorde!* Enough with the yard work, *it's time to make love!* I'm tired of waiting, of planning, of knowing. I'm seizing the day! *Are you ready? Let's go!*

Promises
promises

Yes, I'll be there promptly at eight, I promise. I'll definitely remember to have the kids bathed and dressed in time for the wedding. It's a promise. I promise never to be unfaithful. I promise we'll be together always. Just like I promised, the game will be over and the guys will be gone before your book club arrives. Of course I'll vacuum! Promise! I'll call as soon as I get off the plane. I won't let Mikey do anything crazy to his hair or his belly button. I'll never, ever consider doing anything sexual without protection. Cross my heart and hope to die! Nothing moves forward without your approval—and you have my word on it! We don't need anything in writing: We'll each promise always to be able to sit down and discuss things calmly! Promise me you'll find someone new after I'm gone. Didn't we promise we would take turns cleaning the toilet? I never promised that! I only promised I would con-sider it! Let's promise never to sell the silver, no matter what. Remember when we promised never to make promises? I just broke my promise, so promise me you'll break yours. Promise?

Sanctuaries

In the woods, beside the creek. High on the mesa, beneath the ruins. Down in the cellar, behind the furnace. At his desk, late on Sunday. Back at the woodpile, chopping, chopping. Out on the range, running the horses and racing the wind. Over at the levee, skipping stones. Hangin' at the garage, tinkering with tools. Men without women. Men deep within. On the floor of the library, flipping through picture books. Up on the roof, watching the sunset. At the tip of the island, building castles in the sand. Down on his knees, surrounded by Spirit. Underwater. Alone in his den, gathered at the lodge. Lost in his music, seeking the silence. Finding his song, quelling the voices. Behind the wheel. At the controls. On the road. Off the grid. Below the surface. Beyond the din. Far away, men go within.

Wheels

Cars! Trucks! Motorcycles! Bikes! Skates! Trains! When a man feels like life's driving him crazy, nothing settles like his favorite set of wheels. He slips in behind the wheel, and he rides into the wind on his trusty steed. He slides under the wheels with a wrench and a rag, and the rest of the world fades away. Waxing and polishing and tweaking and torquing. His car is a shrine in the temple of Go! He's always wanted wheels. He watched fire trucks and dump trucks and freight trains and never got enough. He made trucks out of empty oatmeal boxes and coasted to a soapbox victory, and corralled his first car the day he turned sixteen. Two wheels, four wheels, six wheels, a semi! He's riding low to the ground, he's riding shotgun with a friend, he's riding high in style in the old battered pickup of his dreams. Watch him winding down the trail in his fully loaded wheelchair! See him cruising the coast in his comfy sedan! He's just turned forty and he's sporting in his sports car! It's the *wheel* thing! Whoever first invented the wheel, had a man in mind.

Gratitude

gratitude

We are grateful when a man can say *Thank You*. He recognizes when he has been given a gift, and he receives it with heartfelt gratitude. He's learned to say *Thank You* in the most lovely ways, and his gestures are always so welcome. He is thankful that he can wake up and greet a new day, and walk out into the crisp morning air. If he can't walk, he is grateful that he can see yellow daffodils and smell the sweet fragrance of blooming lilacs, and if all he can do is sense the world around him, he is grateful for having that, too. He can receive a compliment without feeling embarrassed and is grateful when someone lends him a hand. He takes nothing for granted without giving thanks, and appreciates all he's been given. He still believes that Thanksgiving is more than a day to watch football, and he offers his thanks before every meal. He'll never forget just how much he's been blessed, and for that we are so very grateful.

Songs
songs

His national anthem. The Yellow Rose of Texas. The lullaby his Nana sang while she rocked him gently to sleep. Semper Fidelis. Amazing Grace. Take This Job and Shove It. The songs they played the summer he lost his virginity. The Christmas carols that blared incessantly in the department store where he worked to earn some pocket money. The song his children say he always sang, but he can't remember the tune. Songs from boot camp and church camp and Boy Scout camp and the camp for boys who just kept screwing up. The solo he sang on stage in the seventh grade, just before his voice changed. Bawdy, raucous, barroom songs, and Ninety-Nine Bottles of Beer on the Wall sung in the back of the bus. Cryin' country songs about love gone bad and life gone sour, and how good men always get left behind. Gospel songs and unchained melodies and the last, booming bars of the Hallelujah Chorus. Lyrics he'll never get out of his head; these songs live on in his heart.

focus

When he wants, if he wants, a man can focus with the absolute precision of a laser. He is calculating the amortization schedule to five decimals, scanning a 269-page report for the errant comma and wayward space, and polishing a 1937 headlamp until it gleams like the eye of a dragonfly. He is mesmerized, watching worms burrow in the compost, lining up a free shot in front of a crowd of twenty-three thousand, looking deeply into your eyes. He hears nothing while he's looking, sees nothing while he's listening, knows nothing else while he coaxes those low, plaintive notes from that battered horn that's been with him forever. It's not that he's gone away—just that for the moment, whatever he's doing, he's purely and sharply in focus.

Work
work

It doesn't matter how many jobs a man may have, unless he's found his work. Not just the work that pays the bills, but the work that feeds his soul. The real work of a man goes on twenty-four hours every day, seven days a week. The work to define his place in the world, and to help create that world. The vocation that fits him like a glove and that no one else can do exactly like him. If he listens, work will call to a man. But until he's found right livelihood, everything else may feel wrong. He can work for money or love or sheer satisfaction. He may wear a white collar or a blue collar or a pink collar or no collar at all. He can work for wages or work for himself, or work for the company store. A man can work with his hands or his head, but to work at what he loves, a man must work from his heart. He must give freely of the gifts that only he can give. Until he steps into his one true calling, a man's work will never be done.

Initiative

He's making the first move before others have even entered the game. The ink on the idea is hardly dry, and he's already got the ball rolling. He sees no sense in holding back, so he's made the first call. Put out the invitation. Blazed the first trail. Someone said *What about lunch?* and while others brainstorm their choices, he's called out for pizza and pie. While the fundraising committee explores its options, he's written a check for a $500 challenge grant. There's always one man who doesn't stand on ceremony when it comes to action. As soon as he hears the words *What if*, he's jumped ahead to *Why not?* and *How Soon?* Mention that backyard decks are a nice thing, and he'll start sketching out plans on the back of a napkin. Bring up the possibility of getting together sometime, and before you know it, he's mapped out a perfect evening—right down to the balmy breeze and the moonlit sky. While others may study and ponder and pause, his initiative puts him out front in an instant.

tools

A man and his tools are not soon parted. He keeps them under lock and key, carefully hung on peg boards against drawings that show their perfect resting places. The smaller ones in drawers and boxes and pouches, in places only he knows. He's got tools for the car and tools for the bike, tools for building and tools for tearing apart, and tools to fix the tools when they're out of alignment. Pipe wrenches and metric wrenches and Allen wrenches, and combos that do a little bit of everything but nothing very well. Band saws and hand saws, hacksaws and backsaws. Mallets and hammers, chisels and awl, thingamajigs and whatchamacallits, and like a surgeon, he knows precisely what to use exactly where. Face it, some men were born to screw. His tools dangle from his belt and from the loops of his overalls, and he wants to find them where he left them. Some men are buried with a ball-peen hammer clutched over their hearts, and why not? In life, he's a fool for his tools.

fragility

Oh, he might talk tough, but he's ready to crumble at any moment. Hit the right button ever so gently, and he'll tremble and shudder and collapse to the core. Outside, he's pointing fingers and naming names; inside, he's quaking in his boots. Outwardly, he's demanding answers and flinging testosterone around the room; inwardly, he's praying that no one sees through his grandiosity to the frightened and lonely man inside. Steal a glance and you'll catch him sniffling at the sappy sitcom he swears he hates. Give him some space and there, you see? The sunlight is starting to shine through the chinks in his breastplate. He might be the last to admit it, but the flick of a feather could crack that veneer. Despite all that armor, he moves with potent agility. Doesn't he know how we so love his flagrant fragility?

Resourcefulness

He can make almost anything out of practically nothing. Give him a couple of paper clips and a wrinkled piece of string, and he'll catch enough catfish for five. If he doesn't have exactly the right tool, he'll make one. He once traveled through Europe on a dollar a day, and came home with cash in his pocket. He knows where to find the world's best day-old doughnuts, and what time the last honey-dipped ones are gone. If he's ever caught in a downpour, he can fashion a designer raincoat out of three plastic garbage bags and a pocket-size stapler. He'll whip up an impromptu dinner with potatoes, a prune, and an egg, and for dessert, he'll do something sweet with sausage. He recycled enough cans and bottles last year to pay for his haircuts. He's saved all kinds of this-and-that, and when he needs one, he knows where he's stashed it. When he wants what he wants, he goes right to the source, and if he wants it again, he resources.

Dances

Few can dance like a man can. Shoes off or shoes on, to a big band or a single drum or the music he hears in his head. Watch him whirl and wiggle, shimmy and sway. He's dancing himself over the threshold into manhood. *It don't mean a thing if he ain't got that swing!* He's dancing with wolves. He's dancing alone in the dark. Fred Astaire in top hat and tails, and John Travolta in a bright white suit. He's undulating wildly at the edge of the mosh pit; he's shuffling stiffly in an ancient Egyptian temple; he's dancing the Beer Barrel Polka with Great-Aunt Bertha, and they're still going strong after thirty-five rounds. A man's dance is a lot more than footprints on the floor and a one-two-three-four. He's dancing the ancestral dream in a twenty-pound plumed headdress. He's shaking off his demons and crushing them under the soles of his feet. He's up on the table dancing a striptease, and the kitchen appliances go wild! He's waltzing at the Waldorf and jazzing it up by the jukebox, and no, we can't have this dance, because it's totally his.

*I*ntegrity

When it comes to some things, it's all black and white with not even a hint of gray. He stands firmly on principle, and he's not about to back down. He would never consider lying—and that includes the little white ones. He would never snitch on a friend, because, well, he just wouldn't. He subscribes to a rigid code of honor that he created himself, and don't expect that he'll ever crack it. It's integrity that helps him stay upright when others don't have a leg to stand on. It's integrity that gives him the intestinal fortitude to walk away from the table no matter how seductive the stakes may seem. There's not a single snag in his moral fiber, and his scruples lie close to the bone. He believes in compromise right up to a point, and it's useless to ask him to cross it. His integrity is intact and inherently sound, and if you think that he'll budge, you're mistaken.

Smarts

He's as smart as a whip and twice as fast. He does the times tables while he's waiting for the train, and he loves to play with the pi of a plate. He always starts his crossword puzzles in ink, and never, ever checks the answers until he's thoroughly through. He's got enough street smarts to keep him out of trouble, and enough tree-smarts to keep him out of the poison oak. He's got multiple degrees from the school of hard knocks, and it's hard to know how he knows what he knows, but he knows it. He's on top of current events and celestial events and could write ten thousand words on the events leading up to the Spanish-American War. When it comes to global economics, he's got it down pat. When the buzz is on the Beatles, he knows where it's at. He can reassemble a motherboard in two minutes flat. He's smarter than your average bear, and his pursuit of intelligence is not at all trivial.

Determination

Once a man sinks his teeth into something with dogged determination, no one and nothing can pry it away. He's terminally determined and he just won't quit. He will see the project through to completion, no matter how daunting the obstacles. He is committed to the cause, no matter the odds. He will not take *No* for an answer and he will stop at nearly nothing until he knows he is done. Filled with resolve, a man never wavers. He will cross the finish line with bloodied feet, on his hands and knees if he must, but he will not give up. Who cares what the polls say? He will stay the course and leave no stone unturned. When others say the well is dry, he will find the way to squeeze out one more precious drop. When others are ready to pack it in, he is newly propelled by a fresh sense of purpose. He stands firm in his determination. His backbone will not buckle, and his will power just won't wilt.

Ego

He's got to have a little, but it doesn't have to be the size of Montana. Without an ego, a man could just lie down in front of the door and invite people to walk all over him morning, noon, and night. Without an ego, why would he work out on the treadmill or dress in anything more sophisticated than a paper bag from Bloomingdale's? Properly handled, enlightened self-interest has its place. Ergo, the ego. We love a man with healthy self-esteem, but we'd rather him not have illusions about being the Shah of Iran. We're inspired by a man who looks out for number one—until he forgets the other sixty-seven of us. We love it when a man takes pride in his appearance—but sometimes we need to get to the mirror, too. A well-balanced ego can mean the difference between a man who takes care of himself and a man who worships the very ground he walks on. But when ego expands into sheer egotism, face it, that's when we're gone!

Systems

He's got a modus operandi for practically everything. He can shower, shave, and dress in under eight minutes, with a thirty-second leeway if he doesn't wash his hair. He can feed an entire cafeteria full of kids in twenty-three minutes, because he's got a system. His Standard Operating Procedure says cleats never touch the carpet, boots go to the basement, and slippers always end up beside his easy chair. He plays blackjack and wins, thanks to his system. He plays the numbers when it comes to sales, and more often than not, he's the state's top performer. He's gained less than three pounds and two inches in the past fifteen years, and it's not starvation—it's his system. As a rule, he does drinks on a first date, dinner on the second, and dancing on the third. He follows guidelines that say *Let your heart be your guide* and if his system crashes, he'll just start a new one.

Sillies
sillies

He's got 'em, and he's got 'em bad! Chopsticks up his nose and painting faces on his toes, and a case of the giggles that just won't quit. Trying to whistle with a mouthful of crackers, and cracking up. Teaching the dog to sing harmony to his high school fight song. Turning the silverware drawer upside down and building a city made of potatoes and carrots and knives and forks. *Uh oh, he's bringing out the camcorder and taping the inside of everybody's nose.* But first, he's doing Andy Kaufman lip-synching the theme song to Mighty Mouse on the very first Saturday Night Live. He's doing Rambo with a Yiddish accent, telling knock-knock jokes to Forrest Gump with a Texas drawl. Now he's pulled his T-shirt up and he's dirty dancing on the coffee table while Donna Summer breathes heavily on the radio. It's the Olympics of silly, and he's just scored a 10.

Wanderlust

A man's gotta go when a man's gotta go. The warning signs start popping up months in advance. He's coming home late because he stopped at the travel agent to see the slide show on Bora-Bora. The mailbox is filled with pamphlets from Seattle, Maine, Texas, and Mexico. He's surfing the Web 'til 3 A.M., checking out hostels in the Himalayas, bus connections to Manitoba, barges to Bangkok. Every bag and pack and suitcase is pulled down from the attic and up from the basement for inspection, cleaning, and repair. He's at the library leafing through old copies of *National Geographic*, and there's a stack of travel guides toiletside. Suddenly, he wants to speak Spanish! The phone bill soars; he is calling his brother's old girlfriend's cousin on Cyprus and researching weather conditions in Costa Rica. He digs out his passport and considers getting shots. We're not going to lose him: He just needs to wander!

gadgets

Gadzooks, he's got gadgets! They're in his pockets and on his belt and in a pile by his bed and his chair. Clipped on and strapped on and snapped on, and all too often, slipped out of his sight. Rings full of keys for what he can't remember, and electronic date books so he doesn't forget. When he's not being beeped or vibrated, he's calculating square roots and the power of nine. He's taken over the coveted corner coffee shop table, and neatly arranged his laptop and phone. When he gets an idea, he'll just micro-record it. He's got an electronic whatzit to help him find studs, and an underwater pager that calls in the pike. He's Jean-Luc Picard, raising his phaser and locking his car and defending the star fleet. He's got a timepiece of sorts that he wears on his wrist, but to call it a watch just will not compute. His pocket knife's so loaded that his pocket's overloaded—and the time on his VCR is still flashing twelve. There's just one thing missing, and this would be it: He'd gladly give up gadgets for some batteries that fit!

*I*dealism

Idealism becomes a man. His eyes take on a different shine when he refuses to believe anything but the best in himself and others. His energy crackles when he proclaims that he'll get into the college of his choice—even though he's carried a C average most of his life. His skin glows when he predicts that, this time, love will win out—even in the face of age-old hatred and ignorance. He seems to walk a bit taller when he believes that he can take on the giants of industry and win. He wants to fill a stadium with men of all ages and colors and faiths, and when people say *It'll never happen*, he says *Watch me*. He is a David in a sea of Goliaths, and his slingshot is primed. Send him to Washington and he'll change the system from the inside out! Finance his latest invention and he'll guarantee a 25 percent return! Build a better mousetrap, build a field of dreams, build a bridge in the middle of a desert, and the world will beat a path to your door at $6.50 a head. He won't play dirty, won't play cheap: The way that he plays is ideal.

Fertility

This is not about sperm counts. This is about the potent fruitfulness that lives in a man. It lives in his fertile imagination, in his prolific mind, in the seeds of innovation and initiation that he gently scatters like milkweed in the wind. A man's heart is fertile when it gives rise to acts of perfect love and radical forgiveness. When it sows the seeds of peace and justice. When it flowers and drops its petals in receptive soil strengthened by the sun and nourished by the rain. A man walks upon fertile ground when his every thought and his every action favor compassion over contempt, and amity over animosity. This is more about productivity than it is about reproduction. This is about begetting a future void of old, obsolete ideas, and bringing forth new ways invigorated by new truths. This is about creating; this is about life.

letters

Let the letters begin! Long, chatty, newsy letters, typed out and spell-checked and crammed full of everything that's new and noteworthy. Scribbled chicken scratchings of a letter, written over three days with four different pens, on lined yellow legal paper folded six times to fit the envelope. Dear John letters, Dear Jane letters, terse and tight and to the point. Love letters that spill out on page after page, a shower of moonlight and roses and full-hearted promises. Fountain-penned on creamy laid paper, scented and licked, and *yes!* melted wax! Lonely letters from the front, painting pictures beyond imagination and begging for the tiniest news bits from the normalcy of home. Feather-light letters from the tip of Cape Horn and letters filled with sand and shells and sunshine from the tip of Cape Cod. Letters he wrote and never sent. Letters he received and promptly burned. Airmail and email, every word of it, he-mail.

Freedom
freedom

Nothing can stop a man when he is truly free. He'll quit a six-figure desk job to farm forty acres in Missouri, and never even look back. He'll trade the mini-van for an RV big enough for the whole family, and pack up the kids and the grandparents and the dog and the hamster, and turn life into one free-wheeling family circus. He'll stop writing business plans and start writing his novel. Hair in a ponytail? You bet. Suit and tie? If he wants. He'll wake up one day and realize that he's not a boy anymore, and tell his Dad once and for all that he doesn't want a piece of the family business and never did. He'll sell his golf clubs, his tennis racket and his antique gun collection, and invest in clay and marble and studio space. He'll run the dog before he reads the mail, talk to his God before he calls his broker, and choose to watch a living sunrise over anything that comes out of a dead box. He will live his truth, his own truth, and nothing but his truth. And the truth shall set him free.

Shaving

Watching a man shave is always better than watching television. First, he'll probably wear nothing but a towel. And second, you get to stare at his face without him asking, *What are you looking at?* Then it really gets good. If he appreciates his face as much as you do, he'll start by washing with a gentle soap that he lathers up and massages into his skin. After rinsing, he'll lather up with a badger-fur shaving brush, massaging his face again with loving strokes that go back and forth and around in lazy, languid circles. (If you want to write your initials in the shaving cream or play a quick round of tic-tac-toe, this would be the time). Otherwise, maintain your dignity while he runs the razor up and down his skin in (guess what?) strokes of various lengths and angles. More rinsing, a pat on the cheeks, and some gentle moisturizer applied with fingers that never pull and never scratch. Next time, ask to help.

Journey

When a man goes on his true journey, it's hard to know who might return. For his quest requires that he strip down to his authentic core, that he litter his pathway with the baggage he no longer agrees to carry. He will pass through uncharted territory with no map and little understanding of where he's headed. The trees will be covered with thorns. Large, lumbering dragons will appear without warning and breathe hot fire into his face. Winds will shift and golden fruit will hang just out of his reach when he is starving most. It is a pilgrimage he must make alone, though able guides are recommended. He begins when he is ready. When he can no longer tolerate who he's become. When his only choice seems to be: implode or explode. Loved ones, wait patiently. When the journey's complete, the pilgrim is reborn.

Ease

Sometimes a man is marked by his ease. There's no push, no strain, no struggle. His very presence is as comfortable as an old easy chair and as restful as a sunny day in June. It's easy for him to be with others, because he's found a certain ease with himself. No matter where he goes or what he's doing, he seems to radiate ease. It simply oozes out of him in a gentle way. It's not just that he's an easy-going guy: he's easy-being, too. He's easy to talk to and it's easy for him to listen. He eases into new situations with every hair in place, and you never, ever see him sweat. He makes it all look so effortless—and when he explains it, it sounds so simple, too. While storm clouds gather all around him, he flies through the air with the greatest of ease. All the while, he makes things easy for the rest of us, without making things hard on himself. It looks so easy when he does it! Yet ask him about it and he just might answer: *Ease isn't always so easy.*

Memories
memories

He remembers it like it was yesterday. He was with his father, they were playing checkers, and he triple-jumped his Daddy for a stupendous victory. He was delirious! He didn't understand why Dad got so mad or why he stayed that way for so long. It was the summer before junior high school, and he was playing at the beach. A freckle-faced girl with ribbons in her hair came by, giggling with her friends, and he felt something warm and tingly that he had never felt before. He told his Mom about it, and she told him never again to think such filthy thoughts. His platoon was taking a village, and the sounds of crying women and children nearly drowned out the drone of the jets. Gym class was over, and it was time to hit the showers, and suddenly half the football team circled him and pointed and laughed. He remembers the first-time softness of skin against his own; the blustery day they got the color TV; the sweet, tart taste of his grandmother's blue-ribbon cherry pie. Some things he'll never forget.

Exuberance

exuberance

Look at him go, he's exuding exuberance! Knocking homer after homer out of the park, bounding around the bases at top speed and hand-standing his way into home. He's bouncing for joy at the good news, throwing small children into the air and catching them while they scream with glee. He's giving pink carnations to everyone in the office, just to share his joy. Shaking hands with every person he sees at the station. Calling *Good Day* to strangers galore. He's leaving a trail of laughter behind him, creating a wave of smiles and good cheer. At the coffee shop, it's a round of java and blueberry muffins on him, and the waitress gets 40 percent. Could it be? He's attempting a bit of Michael Jordan in the cereal aisle, leaping over grocery carts and artfully dodging the lunch time traffic. Exuberant? Exactly! Overflowing is he! Just one of the ways that we love him to be.

quirks

He washes his hands at the kitchen sink, but never in the bathroom. Always puts his keys on the hook by the door, with the cut side facing east. Wears linen to eat Italian but never Chinese. Sits down on the toilet. Always. Religiously reads the sports section first, then news, then weather, then the obituaries. Writes exclusively with a roller-tip pen and only signs his name in blue. Wears socks to bed even in summer. Stirs coffee three times and lays his spoon at a 63-degree angle to the mug. Obsesses over pesky nose hairs. Flosses after the first commercial break, and finishes by the third. Folds his 20s, but crumples his 10s. Calls out *On Donner, On Blitzen* during sex. Feeds the fish before absolutely anything, and refuses to pick up the phone on the first ring. Never throws away a single sock, no matter what. Loves to chew on your left ear, but never, ever, your right. Plays Follow the Queen every time he gets the deal. Always opens high, always folds fast.

logic

It only stands to reason. When a man gives his left brain the reins, he can think with impeccable logic. He'll process data like he was born with a chip in his shoulder, and never foot-fault on faulty assumptions. He'll start to spout syllogisms in his sleep. He'll rely on deductive reasoning and inductive reasoning, and never be swayed by seductive reasoning. He'll put two and two together and come up with five, and then posit a hundred theories that prove why he's right. Objectively speaking, his logic would rock Mr. Spock to his Vulcan core. Premise: Never argue polemics unless you're prepared to be pummeled. Premise: Never assume that the irrational is fashionable. He may seem without rhyme, but he's definitely not without reason. Twisted logic makes him tense; invalid lemmata are an indecent proposal. There's a method to his madness, and it's purely scientific. Subjectively speaking? He's not.

Stance
stance

Every man is a giant when he stands up for the truth. We look up to him when he puts his paycheck on the line and refuses to lie about the firm's hiring practices. When he turns in his long-beloved badge in protest that justice is not being served, we are strengthened. We know it takes courage to take a stand against violence, to pull aside another man and tell him how frightened his wife and children have become. When he wheels his chair to the front of the room and demands access to his favorite restaurant, we know that stance has nothing to do with standing on one's own two feet, and everything to do with standing on principle. He shows his true colors when he takes his buddy's keys out of one hand and a bottle out of the other, and walks him home in the rain. When he risks his own comfort to stand in solidarity beside a man he's never met, and faces his greatest fears to hold fast to what he knows is right, we rise to our feet to stand by him with pride.

Questions
questions

What's for dinner? What's the score? Who's on first? What do women want? Do you like it when I touch you here? Do you know where my sunglasses are? Whose day is it to pick up the kids? Should I pick up the cleaning? Guess who just got a raise? Did you hear what they're doing in Washington now? Do you have any idea how much I love you? Where do we keep the vacuum cleaner? How come we always run out of toilet paper? Why can't you leave it alone already? Could you please stop interrupting and listen to me? Who would have thought we'd still be together after all these years? May I call you again? Really, don't you think you'd be happier with someone else? Do I have any messages? What do you mean, "We're lost"? What do you mean, "It's my fault?" Whose razor is this in the bathroom? Do you think I'm getting fat? Do you think this is easy for me? Could we do that again? How could we not? Why me? Why now? Why this?

know-how

A man has a knack for knowing how. He doesn't know it all, but he seems to know a lot. Like how to remove a hook from the mouth of a fish without ripping everything to bits. How to clean the bathroom from ceiling to floor with a bar of soap, and not even leave a single hair behind. And how to take out a tick from the skin of a dog. Something in a man knows how to rub two sticks together to make fire, if he'll let himself remember. He knows how to parent with strength and compassion, if he'll remember a lot of what he forgot, and forget at least some of what he remembers. A man somehow seems hard-wired to know how to put in the batteries, without ever looking at the diagram. He knows how to troubleshoot, without even seeing the chart. He knows how to care for his own well-being, if he'll only give himself the chance. He knows how to live his life from the heart, but he first might have to forget much of what he's been told, and go with what he knows that he knows.

Wildness
wildness

A man will not thrive without his wildness. It lies dormant in his belly, suffocated by dark suits and windowless offices, by too-long days indoors and too-bright nights where no stars can be seen. A man's wildness needs air that tastes clean in his lungs, and open spaces and the vanilla-butterscotch smell of a live stand of pine. He needs to swim with alligators and lunch with monkeys and wake to the dawn's early light. A man's wildness thirsts for an endless sky and hungers for the sight of bear beyond the clearing. He needs the chance to run across the plains, to watch eagles soar and to run barefoot on sun-baked red clay. A man needs the sea and a sudden squall, and the knife-like sharpness of a wind-driven storm across his face. A man whose wildness is intact need not rage to be free. He needs only grit his teeth and howl with coyote, and remember who he was before he became so civilized that he forgot. Forgot about his wildness, forgot how to be wild.

Discipline

No, not the old-fashioned kind based on *Go stand in the corner until you change your attitude, young man!* Real discipline that guides a man to greater balance. That helps him keep his priorities in order. Like meditating twenty minutes every day regardless of what's going on around him. Unplugging the phone and writing every morning, even when he's sure he doesn't have anything to say. Getting out of the city three times a month, without fail. Keeping sacred the time he spends with the children, even during the company's busiest time of year. Getting out for that mid-morning walk whether it's sunny or not. Sticking to just one piece of pie (without whipped cream!) when he'd really rather have two with all the trimmings. Keeping up with his medication every day, although he's feeling fine. Staying away from old addictions, even though he's feeling lousy. Saying *Yes* because he wants to, and saying *No* because he doesn't. A disciplined man takes care of his own needs first and foremost—no matter who is clamoring for him to take care of theirs. He's grounded by his own discipline, and he can stay out as late as he likes!

Hair

Like Sampson, a man can get lost in the power of his hair. Long, dark, wavy hair, short and spiky metallic hair, kinky, nappy, standing-up-like-Kansas-summer-wheat-field hair. A carrot top, flattop, Mohawked, and James Dean-ed and left to tumble where it may. Salty and peppery, great white shocks of Einsteinian splendor, thin and wispy and vainly combed sideways and ordered to "Stay!" Stitched on, glued on, plugged-in hair, slicked back, or wildly frizzed. The wet look, the dry look, the sleepy-shaggy-dog look. And yes, absolutely, the bare-headed elegance and unmistakable sex appeal of no hair at all. Hair on heads, arms, legs, chests, backs, peeking out of ears and noses, tickling the tops of lips and toes, and sneaking out of bathing suits and baseball caps. Dreadlocks, forelocks, curly locks, ponytailed and proudly braided, hair today, gone tomorrow. Long wavy locks swept back from his face. What's left of the leg hair he shaved for the race. *It's coming out by handfuls all over the place!* Coarse and matted, silky, fine! *His hair is so great; I wish it were mine!*

poetry

The soul of a poet comes out in many different ways. He may put pen to paper or form to clay. He may send cards when he's away, strings of words and symbols and stick figures haphazardly arranged in a manner most poetic. He may write verse or sonnet, limerick or lyric, or build a hogan or plant a spiral garden or dance his rite of passage and express pure poetry in motion. The eyes of a poet see beauty everywhere, and the ears of a poet hear the rhythm of verse and rhyme in every howl of wind or whistle of a train or insistent call of a crow. Spoken from a pure heart, *Roses are red, Violets are blue* can carry the potency and poetry of *But, soft! what light through yonder window breaks? It is the east, and Juliet is the sun!* Take care to know when a poet is in your midst. For he will show you the difference between living a life of poetry, and simply writing rhymes.

Buns

Behind every great man is a great behind. Squishy and swishy, sculpted in steel, rosy-cheeked and rippling. Straddling the red-seated stool at the ice cream counter or languidly leaning on the backyard fence. Watch how he sinks into that saddle. His backfield's in motion while he's mowing the lawn. *Must we always giggle when a man's got some wiggle?* Bumping and grinding his bum on the dance floor, and bending over those sweet cheeks when he's stretching before the game. As a tight-end receiver, he kicks butt. With a caboose like that, he ought to have a red warning flag saying *Danger, Curves Ahead!* His hindquarters are handsome, uh-huh! What his keister can do, no other can. *Could those shorts be any shorter? Please?* His derriere is definitely da bomb. Butt out, boy! Shake a tail feather! *Is that a tush behind that bush?* His gluteus draws maximus attention, and the praise is roundly deserved. No ifs, ands, or butts about it. It's the end! The absolute, living end!

Tenderness
tenderness

When a man tends not to be tender, chances are he's pretending. Does he think we don't notice those quiet moments when he is gentle as a fawn? Does he imagine the nurses were too busy to hear him whisper so softly into his wife's ear during her thirty-fifth hour of labor? Could he actually believe they all looked the other way when he held the young boy's hands close in his own, and slowly told the news it was his job to deliver? We know what he does. We know that he pulls over and stops along the highway to bury road kill animals with a prayer; that he gently stroked the silken ears of his best friend as the last sleep overtook her; that he murmured a Russian lullaby while changing his aged father's soiled bedclothes. Not wanting to stare, we saw him lift his college roommate out of his wheelchair and lower him into the water with the most exquisite care. What a sweet, quiet joy, when a man stops pretending and allows himself to be powerfully tender.

Collections

Rows and rows of souvenir snow globes. Practically everything from every Super Bowl for the past fifteen years. Antique kewpie dolls from carnivals throughout the Midwest, and Christmas ornaments with adult-only themes. Clocks and watches and watches and clocks. The collected works of William Shakespeare and salt and pepper shakers from forty-three states. Matchbooks and boxes from San Fran to Sydney; opium weights in all shapes and sizes; and old stock certificates from the Rio Grande Railroad. Video tapes of every Ed Sullivan show and audio tapes of every Prairie Home Companion. Birds made of wood and glass and feathers and tin, and botanical prints by Audubon. Stereographs and the scopes for viewing them. Autographed photos of famous statesmen. Two entire notebooks of recipes for things made with mangoes, and postcards featuring pink flamingos. First editions of anything by Hemingway or Faulkner, and rifles and muskets from the Revolutionary War. And, lest we forget, an entire wall just for Dorothy and her little dog, too.

Presence
presence

How we feel gifted when a man is truly present. Eye to eye, heart to heart, tête-à-tête. Right now. Right here. Fully engaged in the moment and distracted by nothing. When he possesses presence of mind, we are comforted. When he expresses presence of spirit, our spirits are exalted, too. Away from the clatter of beeps, bells, and rings, we are rapt and wrapped up in his presence. A man with presence can captivate an entire room, no matter how short he is or how plain he appears, or how unimportant he's presumed to be. All that matters is that he be present. Remarkably, incredibly present. His gaze is steady, his voice is sure, he hangs on every word and attends to every gesture. This very instant. This very day. Ask what we want most of all from a man. We love it when he gives us presence.

Excitement
excitement

He's so psyched he can't even sit still! Words are tumbling out of his mouth so fast he can barely keep up with himself, and he's doing that little shadow boxing dance around the room! He's dropping to the floor and doing pushups! He's speed-dialing everyone he knows at warp speed! He's whooping and howling and pumping the air with his fists! *Yes!* he cries out! *Words-we-can't-print-here!* he cries out! He's lip-synching to the soundtrack from *A Chorus Line* and high-stepping every time he gets to the words *One! Singular Sensation!* He's calling out for sushi and breaking out the champagne and the good glasses. *(Actually, he's so excited he broke two glasses and then dropped the entire bottle of champagne!)* He can't hide his excitement for a minute! It's right there in front for all the world to see, written all over his, *er*, face! He's jazzed up and worked up and riled up and wound up! There's much ado about something, and his excitement won't quit!

Insight

A man who looks inward discovers an unseen world of understanding. He looks at his childhood with an air of detachment and gains a new awareness for the way he interacts with other men, and with women. He takes a good, hard look at the way he moves through his days and nights, and he gets a fresh perspective on why it all feels so meaningless and pale. He reflects without analyzing. He sits on a hill at the edge of town, staring at a row of fast-moving clouds and pondering the struggles he's endured. Suddenly *Aha!* it all comes together with a resounding click. He hits forty and realizes he can no longer live someone else's life, and the puzzle pieces fall into place. Fuzzy edges become clearly in focus. His perceptions of himself and others take on a new clarity. It's as plain as the nose on his face and he wonders why he never saw it before. He gets what they mean when they say *You don't get it!* and what's more, he gets that he *does!*

Surrender

When a man decides that it's time to let go, it's a pleasure to see him surrender. He stops resisting, ceases the struggle, and instantly realizes how good it feels to stop banging his head against the wall. He has acknowledged that he hasn't got a clue, and that he no longer is grasping to get one. He's ready to accept that his plan is not working, and he'll get out of the way so another plan can. He's been holding back a landslide forever, it seems, and he's spent and he's so very tired. Like a fish, he now knows that you can't fight the river. Instead, he's decided to go with the flow. We watch his fingers slowly unclench and unfold, as he opens his heart to a new way of receiving. He'll step back so something better can come forth. He's ready to give over his personal will, and by doing so, he'll find greater power. When a new wind blows through, it's a sigh of release, when at last he says *Yes, I surrender*.

Wonder
wonder

It's wonderful when a man is filled with wonder! He'll sit on the grass for hours and watch chipmunks in a meadow and peer into the heart of a wildflower, and simply marvel at the wonder of it all. It's wonderful to see wonder in a man's eyes. To see him mesmerized by the sweep of a hundred-year-old suspension bridge, or captivated by the symmetry of a spider's web. To wait and watch while he counts fifty-seven rings in the trunk of a fallen tree. To see him cross-legged on the floor, with the pieces of the ancient engine spread out around him, and he's shaking his head in wonder. He wonders about nature, about God, about man. It boggles his mind and sets his senses reeling, and he can do nothing but wonder. He raises the question *Did you ever wonder?*, content in not knowing the answer. He dives into the future and digs through the past, and he never ceases to wonder. Watch him and see the most wonderful thing: He's wading through a wonderland, awash in the wonder.

Joie de Vivre

He's dedicated to a joyful life, and it's a joy just watching him live it! He'll dress up in his favorite finery and dance half the night, and walk home beneath a blanket of stars. He sees a sky full of silver linings, and never bothers to notice the clouds. He's got no use for news, since it tends to depress him, and he won't sing the blues, because yellow's his tune. He took his watch off in 1975, and is blissfully punctual every-where he goes. He rarely thinks about tomorrow, because the here and now is so utterly delightful. He fills his days with work that he loves and people he adores, and feels blessed every moment he's living. He's joyfully lavish or joyfully simple, dining five-star or grazing at the counter. His favorite dictum is Live Long and Prosper, and he plans to do both quite exceedingly well. His enjoyment of life is a lesson worth learning: Life is for living, so live it with joy!

Taste
taste

Sweet and salty with a hint of spice. Ambrosia of the gods. Almond soap and vanilla lotion with just a touch of ginger. Garlic, chipotle peppers, butter-drenched corn on the cob, and last night's lasagna. Spearmint, peppermint, cinnamint, wintergreen. Honey bees and honeysuckle and fresh hay in the barn. Good, honest sweat and whatever he threw on to hide it. Swimming pool. New car. A cigar? Clean river rocks baked in the sun; quickly falling snow; a warm, cozy fire, and boots in the hall. Today and yesterday and tomorrow and tomorrow and tomorrow. Spiritual man, rational man, Neanderthal man, early man, and man not yet born. Just a dash of the woman inside every man. The mountains at sunrise, the beach at midnight, and the desert just before dawn. Pungent and ripe and raw and bold, the taste of a man is a flavor to savor.

vanity

While some men never pick the crumbs out of their beards, lovable others keep us waiting outside the bathroom while trimming wayward whiskers and pushing back cuticles with surgical precision. (Like *you've* never fussed with your hair for twenty-three minutes only to dunk your head in the sink and start all over? *You've* never put your own chin under a high-beam flashlight to ferret out that stray black-head before it becomes a raging volcano?) Give the guy a break. He's only human, and anything this side of psychopathic narcissism is pretty much a go. Watch him when he looks in the window of the electronics store. Is he really just checking his crow's feet? Count your blessings that he's lavishly lubricating his chapped lips, and lovingly lapping up moisturizer by the liter. He owns three identical suits in three different sizes to flow with his fluctuating weight—and you know you wish you had thought of it first! He's so vain, he probably thinks this page is about him.

Candor

Let's not pull any punches here, okay! To be brutally honest, a man can tell it like it is, like nobody's business. He'll call a spade a spade, even if it's really a shovel. He's the first to tell the manager that the music was awful, the food was cold, and the server was surly. (And he smiles the whole time.) Ask him what he thinks of your hair, and he'll suggest you hold that question until after you've combed it. Give him a taste of your grandmother's famous fruitcake, and prepare yourself for a barrage of comments concerning doorstops, cannon ammunition, and patio construction. He doesn't like what the police department is doing about road rage and he'll be happy to spout off about it to the first cop he sees. He'd rather shoot the Colorado rapids than visit the Nebraska pioneer museum, and he's not about to pretend otherwise. Don't expect him to walk on eggshells when the truth begs to be told. He'll raise his sword high and cut clean through the chaff, and leave us totally smitten with candor.

Music

The very best music is the music a man makes himself. Drumming a steady beat on the lunchroom table, jingling a jangle of keys in his pants pocket, whistling while he waits for the waitress to bring his BLT. Arias in the shower and air guitar in the garage. Was that Sinatra in the cab of his truck? Cradling his mandolin in his arms and strumming a lullaby for baby; picking out a polka on his great-uncle's accordion and begging his Boobie not to cry. Blowing Taps at the funeral of a fallen hero without flinching an inch. Happily obliging a request for anything at all by Dylan. Anything at all by Monk. Turning his eyes toward heaven and lifting his voice in praise. When a man has a song in his heart, it won't be long before he pulls a harmonica out of his boot, or lovingly lifts his violin from its battered case. Listen as he tickles those ivories! It will sound like he's making love to the world, when a man is loving making his music.

Dreams

I dreamed I was in my car and there was no steering wheel and I just couldn't get to wherever I was going. I called for help and no one answered, and I woke up drenched in sweat and with my heart pounding. I dreamed I was Peter Pan, but this woman in an apron came and clipped my wings and I fell for what seemed like eternity. I don't remember what happened next. I dreamed I was shipwrecked on a desert island inhabited by gorgeous women, and they were all too busy to notice me. I dreamed I was in a roomful of men, sort of like the annual sales meeting, but different. One at a time we were given instructions, and when it was my turn, B-52 bombers filled the sky and I couldn't hear what the man in charge was saying. I dreamed I was doing what I had always wanted to do, and that I had a family that I cherished, and that I was living a kind of Heaven on Earth. When I woke up, I opened my eyes and there I was, lying next to you.

Noises
noises

It's that thing he does with his sinuses that really gets our attention. Part throat-clearing and part nose-blowing and part mating call of the elephants. It reverberates through the bathroom and you can hear him approaching for miles. He clicks and clucks and tickles his tongue against the roof of his mouth and the back of his throat, and cracks his knuckles and toes in a torrent of timpani. Snap, crackle, pop, he's a master at self-chiropractic. He burps in baritone like a barbershop quartet, and he can still hold his own with that underarm blatting in the swimming pool. His snoring is a cacophonous symphony of snorting and snuffling, with wheezing and whistling thrown in just for show. How he hacks and hiccups through hay fever season! How he gurgles and gargles post-garlic! His repertoire ranks with the truly fantastic, but the best noise of all is when he's wildly ecstatic.

Color

Spare us the monotony of dark blue suits and red power ties! Give us crimson and vermilion, gamboge and cerulean, olive drab and olive divine. Bright swatches and pale washes, cascading over shirts and sweaters and onto flowing silk jackets. Muted palettes, tone on tone, chalky, dusky, deep, and dark. Ebony and alabaster, brilliant contrast is what we're after. *(Did you see that man wearing all that violet? Check out that pair of scarlet shoes! Oh, for a blonde in UPS brown! Oh how we cry for mouth-watering hues! And while we're on the subject we're on, why so seldom celadon?)* Terra cotta makes khakis crackle. A touch of teal gives salmon snap. Healing blue and golden spirit. To tune up your spectrum, first you wear it! Red for grounding and green for the heart. Life is a canvas and a man can be art!

Fears
fears

Believe what you like, but terror sometimes stalks the heart of a man. He is deathly afraid of dying, of losing his youth and his vigor, his vim. He can't shake loose of the fear that someone or something, somehow wants to reel him in and tie him down and shove a cold, hard bit into his mouth. Believe what you will, but a man is so afraid of a woman. He fears he will lose his mind under her enchanted spell, that he will lose his balance and be swallowed up by a tsunami wave of womanly wiles. That she will, eventually, see him for what he is, and leave him brokenhearted. A man without work can become nearly paralyzed by fear. He feels without identity, without means, without stature, and fears he is invisible. You can believe what he tells you, but know this is true: A man lives in fear of his fears.

Voice

Listen to the voice of a man. Hear it cry out for freedom and call out in triumph. Hear it keen and bellow and moan and wail. His is the voice that exploded in battle; his is the howl that ignited the flame. Beneath all the babble, he spoke sotto voce; his basso profundo enveloped the hall. You can hear the entire world in the voice of a man. The bit of brogue, the touch of twang, the patois of the plain, and the elocution of the noble. The changing voice of a boy becomes the unwavering voice of a man. A full-throated man voices his fears and his deepest yearnings. He voices his anger as he voices his joy. If called upon and ready, he voices the conscience of the people. The strongest men's voices still strain to be heard, while somehow, the lesser are heard over all. Listen to the sound of a man's voice in all of its glory. It just might be an angel, with the voice of a man.

Commitment

commitment

What's all this talk about fear of commitment? He signed up for two post-graduate degrees and $100,000 in loans, and he's committed to seeing them all the way through. He signed on as a soldier in the middle of a war, and that's a commitment you don't walk away from. He spends every single Sunday with some boys from the shelter, and he knows how they'd feel if he failed to show up. His personal commitment is to heal his home planet, and he gave away his car to prove that it's real. He's committed to improving public education and he's in the classroom every week, helping kids learn to read. He tithes his income every year without fail. He's building a center for injured birds of prey, and he'll keep going until it's completed. He's committed himself to the people he loves, and they know they can trust his commitment. He's focused on what counts, and he won't be derailed, and that's the true sign of commitment.

Excess
excess

He's too much! He drives too fast and laughs too loud, and given the chance, he'll sleep too long! He's over-worked and over-stressed and over-sexed and don't look now, but he's head-over-heels in love again! Once is never enough, and sometimes he can't stop himself. If the recipe calls for two eggs, he'll throw in four just for good measure. If there's a chance of rain in the forecast, he'll hose down the car and put out the sprinkler. *What? We're out of pretzels again?* He's over the top! He gives too much on birthdays, volunteers too many hours to help the homeless, and is way ahead of himself when it comes to phone trees for third-world causes. He buys too many lunches for too many people at work, and does all the cooking for everybody at home. Sometimes he calls eight times a day just to say *I miss you*—and then he follows up with emails galore just to say it again. It all seems like excess, but think this one through: Without it, he'd be so exceedingly bland!

Nerve
nerve

Call it *pluck* or call it *chutzpah*, but a man is a bundle of nerve. It takes nerve to stand up at the Thanksgiving table and tell the family you're not going to hide their dirty little secret anymore. Or to tell your dying grandmother you're going to prison and probably won't be out in her lifetime. You've got to have guts not to look the other way like everybody else. To blow the whistle on corruption and take the glare of the television cameras and the white heat of the courtroom. It takes cojones to be the only gay man or straight man, or Jew or Muslim, or white or black or Cambodian man in a sea of other brothers. A man's gotta have more than a little moxie to join an all-woman organization, sign up to pour the tea, and then date the president, to boot. Sometimes, the nervy man asks *Why?* Other times, he audaciously asks *Why not?* Either way, they're going to say *Man, he's got some nerve!*

Stories
stories

How a man can weave a fine yarn! He'll have you gripped with suspense over his harrowing tales of backpacking in the outback, extortion in Latin America, and that long, long, first step off the side of an ice-covered mountain. You'll be rolling with laughter when he recounts the whole sordid saga of the morning he locked himself out of the house in his altogether, just in time for the arrival of the garbage trucks. He'll intrigue you with the details of his summer on an Israeli kibbutz, building irrigation ditches and dodging bullets in the blazing sun. He'll pull at your heartstrings with stories of unrequited love. He'll knock your socks off with wild and fanciful stories of liaisons interruptus and magical myths explaining the appearance of the first man, first elephant, first star in the sky, and last ship to set sail in the storm. Fish story or true confession, a man tells a hell of a tale.

Passion

passion

How we are ignited by a man's passion! It roars through him, red-hot from the base of his spine, until he can contain it no more. Then how he lives! How he throbs with aliveness! How he picks up his paintbrush and covers canvas after canvas! How he wraps himself around his cello and strokes his way to ecstasy! How he writes, page after page, with pencil or crayon, on paper or on the walls if he must! His passion propels him into action with an urgency he cannot deny! He will move mountains on behalf of the children! He will knock on every door to make a clarion call for peace! He will go without sleep for days on end, to follow the path of his passion! He will embrace his God with a newfound fervor, and embrace his beloved with a newly lit fire! He is madly in love with love and with life! Truly smitten is he, he's afire with passion!

Choices

When it mattered most, he chose love over fear and compassion over judgment. He listened to his own intuition rather than the din of voices around him, and from there on, all his choices became easier. Sometimes he flipped a coin, but he made his choices and he lived with them and never had any regrets. After weeks of sleepless nights, he decided to start his own home-based business and pass on the lucrative contract that came with a three-hour daily commute. He chose time over money and less over more. He chose simplicity. Chose joy. He chose to stay and work through the whole mess, even though it would have been a lot easier to walk away. He went with authenticity instead of illusion. He chose reading over television. The future instead of the past. When faced with the choice of losing his family or losing his soul, he chose a way to keep them both. When he knew he had the choice between living his life the "right way" or his way, the choice was so easy, it was no choice at all.

Constancy

There's something in a man that can wash away worry and wonder. When he says he'll be there, you know he will. Some things you can count on like spring following winter and the sun coming up every morning. When he tells you he'll take care of it, you don't need to give it a second thought. He's up every day at 5:43 A.M., give or take a few minutes, and you can set your watch by it. He'll have oatmeal every morning, with two eggs on Thursday and a waffle if it drops below freezing. He'll carry his lunch in his right hand and his newspaper in his left. And you can take that to the bank. He'll never make a promise he can't keep, and never speak a word that he won't later honor. If he says he'll refinish the floors by February, go ahead and send out Valentine's party invitations and trust he'll come through. One thing is certain: He won't be bringing home a lot of surprises, but if it's the second Tuesday of the month, you can definitely count on him bringing home Chinese.

Openness

He's an open book and he's ready to be read. He'll ask you for the time, and the next thing you know, you're connecting like old friends over pie à la mode. Approach him for directions, and he'll reel off a full-length history of the downtown corridor, complete with sound effects. Ask him how he is, and he'll say a lot more than just *Fine*. He'll strike up a conversation in the canned soup aisle, and never stop chatting until you know everything there is to know about his Great-Aunt Louise and her adventures in Hollywood. *Whoa, bro, XYZ!* He listens to Larry King and he's equally fluent in liberal. He'll attend temple on Friday night, a Wiccan circle on Saturday, and a Baptist revival on Sunday morning. Monday, he's back to zazen. His heart is on his sleeve, and chances are good his shirt is unbuttoned. His defenses are down and he's up for conversation. He's peeling off his layers and weeping all the while. His welcome mat is out and his door is open, twenty-four hours a day.

Shorts

Men in shorts deserve a closer look. A much closer look. They wear them over tights and sweat pants, and under most everything else. Long, baggy jams in Hawaiian prints, and khaki camp shorts with pockets for a gaggle of gadgetry. Mud-smeared rugby shorts that somebody yanked down low. Cycling shorts shamelessly stuffed with never-chafe chamois. They're lined up at the start line by the hundreds, long and lean and lanky legs that never seem to stop. *Could you do that stretch just one more time? Once again, now from the top?* He's lounging poolside, legs slouched-eagle over the sides of the chaise, and swim trunks catching a stiff summer breeze. *Ach du lieber! It's lederhosen!* Put on your shades! He's in tennis white! The long and the short of it? Not every man looks smashing in shorts, and there are some knees we don't need to see. But cutoffs cut off within an inch of his life—to make a long story short—are one fine cup of tea.

Radiance

When a man shines from within, the whole world seems aglow! His eyes pierce the darkness like beacons of the soul, and he carries a luminance that can best be described as beatific. How his energy enwraps us and draws us higher; how his inner light beams through his radiant skin. He emits a brilliance of body, mind, and spirit, and his beauty conspires to take our breath away—or perhaps to give it back. We think that he's practically floating on air; that in a pinch, he could walk across water. Whatever he is eating or doing or not, the state of his being cannot be ignored. A radiant man is a man who's alive. He's learned to stay grounded while his spirit can soar. We watch and we wonder where he's gotten his radiance. And we know in our hearts that we wish we had more.

Appetite

Sometimes a man just can't get enough. He wants fries with his burgers and buttermilk with his chowder, whipped cream and maple syrup on his pumpkin pie, and *oh, if you don't mind, could you go a little heavy on the gravy?* He'll have oatmeal before breakfast, last night's leftovers before lunch, and a salami sandwich, pickle, and a brew with the nightly news. He is a modern-day Fred Flintstone slamming down a rack of tyrannosaurus with a triceratops on the side. Take a closer look: He's got appetizers in his attaché and bags of pretzels in his backpack! His head says *Fat-Free* but his appetite cries *Doughnut!* A born hunter-gatherer, he's stalking the aisles for fettuccini and feta, scouring the hills for banana pie filling, and gathering all the bagels and cream cheese he can stick a spear through. When a man is ravenous, one can only stand back. Or, of course, one can choose to be dinner...

empathy

The empathic man is not so hard to find. He is at the office, on the job site, eating a sandwich, chatting on the Internet. He has lived enough life to know how to give. He has opened his ears and his heart to walk a mile in another man's shoes. To meet him exactly where he is right now. He listens without judgment, comforts without advice. He may nod a lot. He may say *I know what you mean* over and over. But mainly, he listens. How can he do otherwise? He's been there, inside the shame and the guilt, imprisoned by the pain and anger, consumed by the fear. He may hold another man's hand, or wipe his brow while he pukes, or keep an eye out so that no one gets hurt. But mainly he's a witness to something he's seen up close and personal. For the moment, he and another man have intersecting lives. What he can offer, and give, is his empathy.

Cravings

He wants some red licorice, and he wants it bad! He's craving his mom's macaroni and cheese, and she's miles away, and nobody else can make it like she can! Suddenly he has to see Dustin Hoffman on screen, but it's Sunday night and all the video stores are closed! What he wouldn't do for beef jerky! He would ransom the family jewels to be lying on a beach right now, this very instant! He has an unscratchable itch to hear Seiji Ozawa and Yo Yo Ma, and he's not even sure who they are! He has this nearly uncontrollable urge to play pinochle, and he thinks it's a French form of poker! If he doesn't get to Vancouver in the next few days, he's going to bust a gut! He's calculating the monthly production figures, but his mind keeps crying out FISHING! He could deal with it all, if only he could have a box of Girl Scout cookies, but it's the middle of November and there are none to be had. *Where is that licorice? He's got to have it now!*

Stillness
stillness

Be aware of a man when he's deep in his stillness. He's turned off his beeper and put down his book and at least for the moment, he's perfectly still. Catch a glimpse of him sitting in the yard taking note of nothing, while the rake and the clippers lie idle. The TV is off and he's sitting by the window, simply staring into unlimited space. He's not doodling or figuring or thumbing through trail guides. His body and mind are both blissfully still. Call it meditation, call it prayer, call it tapping into stillness and listening to that small, still voice within. He's sitting by a tranquil lake and his fishing rod has never wavered, and he's caught a stillness that's filled with all time. He's sitting in his truck at the height of a storm, and he's totally enveloped in stillness. Don't ask what he's doing; he's doing the stillness. He's not doing nothing; he's doing it all.

Directions
directions

Directions? Oh sure, it's really very simple. You go about, oh, 2.6 miles and the road turns left at about a 62-degree angle. You keep on for oh, about 153 yards until you see a wooden fence on your right. There's a driveway after the seventh fence post, although it might be hidden by a low-hanging willow tree. Estimated travel time is about seventeen and a half minutes, give or take 3 percent. You can't miss it. Stay on the road a bit. You'll pass three or four, maybe five lights. Somewhere on your right will be an old bowling alley or maybe it was a roller rink. There's no sign, but you can't miss it. Then a little ways after that, the road veers sort of to the right. Don't go too far or you'll end up at the drive-in. You can't miss it. If you get to the trading post shaped like a tepee, you've missed it. At the fork, take the high road. You'll see some cows and some rocks. There's a dirt road to the right, unless the creek is running high or the cows have wandered. Directions? Wish I could help you out, but I've never thought to ask.

What's more sweet than a man when he's sleeping? Catching forty winks before the concert. *(Honey, get up!)* Napping like a cat curled in the sun on the chair in the southernmost window. *(Sweetie, they're going to be here any minute!)* Sitting up in the driver's seat, legs a-tangle under the steering wheel, head straight back and mouth wide open, ready to jerk awake at the slightest touch. *(Let Daddy rest, he's been driving for hours!)* Schnoozing and snoring and snorting on the sofa after an all-nighter. Dead to the world after double-shifting for a friend. Sleeping like an angel with his hair in his eyes and his lips slightly parted and his legs wrapped up in his favorite blankie. Slumped over his desk, cheeks nestled ergonomically into the keyboard. Sleeping for days because his body said *Stop!* Sleeping because he's exhausted to the core. We tiptoe, we whisper, we check for his breathing. *(Who me? I'm not sleeping! Just resting. Let's go!)*

longing

It's a long way from a man's Glad-To-Meetcha pump of the hand, to the depth of his *longing*. For all his talk about wanting to be longer, in truth he just wants to *belong*. He aches for a kind of connectedness that he has never observed, much less experienced. His longing takes him down pathways that too often leave him longing. He yearns to feel whole. To feel so at home with himself, that he can feel comfortable spending long, intimate hours with others. There's a part of a man that longs to understand. He longs to ask his father *What was it like for you?* and he craves a response that can help him unravel the knotted strands of his own existence. He knows he has a son, and he will never lose the longing to look into that man's eyes and catch a glimpse of himself looking in a mirror. Some men wait a very long time before they let loose their longing. Some wait too long and leave longing still.

Experience

Some men have been around the block more than once—and it wasn't their paper route. He shucked oysters in the East. His heart stopped beating one night, and by the time the doctors got it going again, he had had an out-of-body experience and a near-death experience and a fifty-six-page-bill experience. He was digging some fence holes in his backyard, and a thirty-foot python nearly licked his face. He ran a red light and had to spend the night in jail with three guys who wouldn't stop singing the theme song from the original *Beverly Hillbillies* TV show. He worked his way through college impersonating a mannequin in a department store window—but had to quit when hay fever season kicked in. His mother left him at the hospital when he was born, and he was taken in by a couple in their sixties who adopted fourteen children besides him. He won the lottery once, and as he left the bank with a fat roll of cash, he was beaten and robbed of it all. When he was nine, he tried to fly through a glass window and fell four stories. To this day, whenever he's asked about his experience, he shrugs his shoulders and says *None*.

flaws

Thank goodness for the flaws that make a man human. Better he leave his underwear on the bathroom floor, than leave it somewhere else. Maybe he's home ten minutes late, but at least he's coming home. If his ego is a bit oversized, maybe that's because his destiny is truly grandiose. If his manners are a bit rough, be thankful he's still got some wildness left within. If he won't speak up to your mother, consider that it's not his job. *(So what if he's laconic? You'd rather have a man bionic?)* If he seems a little meek and mild, some would say he'll inherit the earth. Flawless is for diamonds—nice to look at, but pretty cold to curl up next to during winter's long, dark nights. A man is more like a postage stamp with a missing letter: What may seem like a flaw is a mark of rare value. His imperfection is perfect: Just let the man be!

Snuggling

What perfect pleasure to sleep lying snug in the curl of a man! To lay your ear upon his chest; to hear the beating of his heart and feel the rise and fall of his breath. Nothing satisfies quite like snuggling. We fold ourselves into chairs made for one and pour ourselves all over the lawn furniture. Legs intertwined like vines, like ivy climbing up the garden wall. Noses nuzzling like horses in heat; searching out warm spaces for icy-cold feet. Who could turn down an invitation to cuddle up with a good man and a great book and a perfect cup of tea? To wrap arms around necks and burrow bellies up to backs and lay cheek-to-cheek? We curl up and over and around and behind and our hands find their way into round, empty hollows. We embrace outdoors, snuggled against skin made warm by the sun, or lightly moistened in a light, spring rain. We lounge about on park benches with heads in laps and on bosoms and nestled in necks, until everyone around us is snuggling, too.

Needs

A man needs to learn what it means to be a man. He needs to meet his own needs, and to ask for help when he needs it. He needs time with himself and time with others. He needs one or two authentic friends, be they women or men, and he needs to trust them without reservation. A man needs a companion, two-legged or four-. He needs to know his history—who were the men who came before him and which of their needs were never met. He needs to acknowledge that there may be something larger than himself, and he needs to figure out for himself exactly what that might be. He needs to be listened to without interruption, especially when he's having a hard time knowing what to say. A man needs someplace to call his own, and if that place has a door, he's the only one who needs the key. A man needs to know himself inside and out. Sometimes he needs to cry and to laugh, and to know that both are okay. A man needs to know that he's only a man. And he needs to know that is enough.

Respect

A man learns the fine art of respect by practicing on himself. He respects his right to be treated fairly and so treats others with fairness. He insists that others respect him enough to look into his eyes when they speak to him, and to disagree with him without shaming or blaming. He expects respect from his children, yet knows he will earn it only by respecting them in kind. He shows his respect in small ways. By listening without interrupting. By doing his very best to understand. By remembering where others have come from, and how little respect they might have been given along the way. He respects elders for their wisdom, and young ones for their innocence. He respects the fact that he will be judged by his actions, and so forms his opinions of others based on their deeds and not just their words. Knowing that life is short, he pays his respects when people are living, and not just after they've died. He knows the worth of who he is, and so he is worthy of our respect.

Beginnings

First thing Saturday morning, he bought new running shoes and mapped out a ten-kilometer loop around the neighborhood. Before he even had a design, he selected a stunning piece of fabric and ordered hand-carved buttons from India. Before he started cleaning the basement, he put on a fresh pot of coffee. He made the call and set up a lunch date. Sketched out a floor plan and got the names of three architects. Cleared out a space with room to do yoga. Read Genesis for the first time. He notified the adoption agency that he wanted to meet his birth mother. Made an appointment to see an oncologist. He got out the seed catalogs and piled them up by his favorite chair, and reserved a Rototiller for the first weekend after the last frost. He met his newborn daughter for the very first time, and right off the bat, fell in love. He was the first one to speak: He admitted he was in way over his head, and that was the first step. As soon as he finished, that's when he began.

Will

When a man wants to make something happen, he will. He'll stoke his inner fire and direct his energy and create a force to be reckoned with. Once his intention is clear and his will is focused, a man can have what he wants, and do what he wants, and most important of all, he can be who he wants. A man who's found his will, is sure to find his way. But first he must will it to be. He must yearn enough and ache enough until he builds sufficient willpower to act with purpose and move with resolve. He must speak with a willing voice so that others will hear. He must create his motions through sheer sense of will—and let it be known that he's willing. No matter what he wants, a man will be able when he's ready to be willing. First he must will it, and then it will be.

lists

The list of things he'll do today, with stars for priority status. The list of things he never got around to yesterday. The list of people he has slept with—and the (much longer) list of people he wished he had. The list of his significant other's sizes, which he will carry in his wallet at all times and which will mysteriously disappear just before every known holiday. His running list of must-see films. His list of Important Dates to Remember, which he may or may not. The creased and fingerprinted list of ten famous men who became fabulously successful after four, five, or six failings at business. The list of places he would like to visit if he could ever make the time. The list of affirmations given to him by a channeler just outside Sedona, Arizona. The list showing the sodium and fat contents of popular items from fast-food restaurants. The list of books he wants to read, but probably won't get around to. The list of companies he would work for if he ever considered jumping back on the career track. The list of vegetables he'll grow in his garden when he's finally jumped off for good.

Sweaters
sweaters

We're sweet on a man in a sweater. All furry and woolly and soft to the touch. He's as calming as Mister Rogers in a cardigan; as comical as Cosby in a geometric print. He's a Celtic sailor in a fisherman knit, damply wrapped in stretched-out bottom and shapeless sleeves and smelling like salt and sea air. He's wearing a V-neck to celebrate a victory from ties; and his turtleneck lets him crawl into his shell. There's a kaleidoscopic pattern draped across his shoulders, an Icelandic border that runs down his sleeve. He's wearing the tattered sweater his grandmother knit for him, the last cables she could stitch after her eyes quit but her fingers kept going. He still wears his college letter sweater, though it's been thirty-five years since he put the shot out of anyone's range. He's a dyed-in-the-wool lover of sweaters. He's absolutely the best in worsted! Terribly terrific in a sudorific! When a man is embraced by the arms of a sweater, what a pearl of a spell doth his warp and woof weave.

Ears

Here, here, let's hear it for his ears! We love it when they listen. He can hear the thin cry of a feverish baby from two floors away, and the crack of a twig under the paw of a pussycat crossing the lawn in the rain. He can sit in the balcony and hear an errant F sharp from the second violinist, and hear a carburetor ping in the middle of rush hour traffic downtown. *Did you hear that?* he asks, when the blender whines in unfamiliar fashion. In the last moments, he bent over until his ear was practically touching the old wrinkled mouth, and he heard that final *Goodbye*. He was in surgery for sixteen hours, and he heard the doctors laughing at jokes he swears he could hear. When they suggested he get a hearing aid, he wouldn't hear of it—but the things that he heard when he did! He heard laughter and church bells and the cry of the magpie. He heard the whistle of the train and he knew she was gone. How come then, we ask, that he never can hear when we call him to supper, so often and long?

Rhythm

To find his own rhythm, a man needs to discover the beat of his own heart. He begins slowly by taking off his watch, turning off the automatic coffeemaker, and finding the cadence that is his alone. He notices when the sun rises and sets, when the moon swells to fullness, and when the leaves begin to turn. He acknowledges—indeed, *welcomes*—the changes in his body as he ages, and the changes in those around him. In time, he will sense the cycles of ebb and flow that run through every segment of his life, and he will honor them without fear. He will find himself as one drop of water in an ocean of infinity, and he will feel whole. When a man can lie on the ground and feel the heartbeat of Mother Earth beneath his own, he will find himself in sync with the very flow of life itself. The passage of time will take on a new quality; death and rebirth will follow in their turn. Then he is free to add his own beat to the universal pulse. To join in the drumming, the rhythm of life.

Prudence
prudence

He's the one who's patiently waiting for the *Walk* sign before crossing the street, and then looking both ways anyway. He thinks before he puts his mouth in gear, and looks before he leaps, and sometimes chooses not to leap at all. His sense is uncommonly common. Next to him, Smoky the Bear looks like a slacker when it comes to prevention. He visits his dentist two times a year, and never misses his annual physical. He changes the oil before the car starts to smoke, and gets to the roof leaks long before the rain. He's a fiscal conservative and is always the first one to cut his losses. When the sign says *Proceed with Caution*, he does. When the surgeon says *Give this decision the time it deserves*, he will. Run out of gas? Don't be ridiculous! Dead flashlights and no batteries in the house? You obviously have him confused with somebody else. He was born to plan, and as for his dying, the final arrangements have all been arranged.

Fatherhood

There's a moment when a man becomes a full-fledged father, and it's not when his child is born. It's that first night the two of them are alone and he figures out that lying heart-to-heart with a baby is an all-around soother when everybody gets a little colicky. It's being there the first day of kindergarten and the last year of college. It's giving an unqualified *No* to all-night keg parties down by the graveyard, and a tentative *Yes* to the new tattoo. Fatherhood becomes the man who shows up at the school concert even though he's got work to do, and who finds time to play at the playground even though he was invited for tee-off at ten. It's learning the times table together at the kitchen table, and staying up late to read *The Hobbit* out loud. True fatherhood is not how many children a man sires, but whether he has held a child under his wing until the child is ready to fly. It's showing instead of telling, explaining instead of yelling, and knowing that when the time comes, the father becomes the child, and the child becomes the father.

Secrets

Not the ones he keeps bottled inside, but the ones we're privy to. The ones he shares with us and we promise not to repeat. The ones he swears he never told anybody else. Intriguing secrets like that one about what really happened to the principal's car after the Senior Prom. Or the one about his secret Mediterranean rendezvous with someone whose identity must still remain a secret. Secrets from his deepest heart. His secret hopes, his secret passions, his secret dreams. Sweet and charming secrets that make him smile and shake his head in fond remembrance. Childhood secrets that bring on a chuckle. *Guess where Billy's secret agent decoder ring really ended up?* Small secrets that wouldn't seem to matter much, except to him, they do. His secret for growing the juiciest tomatoes in town. His secret recipe for his famous Cajun marinade. His secret strategy for winning at chess every time. And the secrets we never hear? They're in his secret garden, and he's holding tight the key.

odds & ends

A fringe of silken lashes resting on a sleeping cheek. The classic curve of a well-muscled calf. His unwavering adherence to his own healthy boundaries. His understanding of ovulation. Toenail clippings piled neatly on the rec room rug. Mustache trimmings swept neatly into the trash. Frequent restroom stops on the road, even though he doesn't have to, but he knows that you do. His hard-earned status as a card-carrying feminist. His intolerance of any kind of intolerance. The way he adores the children, even though they're not his. Absolute integrity, without exception. Watching him wipe away tears in church. Watching him wipe the kitchen counter in his underwear. The impassioned speech he made on behalf of the big oak tree. The picnic he laid out at the foot of the same. The way the street lights reflect off the top of his head. The way a cummerbund encircles his waist. His cowboy grin, toothpick included. His fascination with all things Asian. The way the sun brings out the sparkle in his eyes. The way he brings out the sparkle in yours.

Scent
scent

Musk and moss and a pine forest sunrise. Red-walled canyons and grass freshly mowed and sheets warm from the dryer or never washed at all. Diesel and motors, paper and wood and ink and feathers and bone. New leather, old leather, leather that his great-uncle wore to war. Bread baking and espresso, incense and eucalyptus, cognac and cigars, citrus of any kind, and yes, tobacco. A light breeze coming in from the coast, shaving cream and soap, or no soap at all. High-grade chocolate made in Switzerland and out-of-this-world frybread made at home. His father's bathroom, his mother's perfume. Baby powder and spit-up milk and diapers dried on the line. Dog, slightly wet. Cattle and horses and the subway and hard work and the smell of an opening heart. Artist's paints in tubes and turpentine and fresh-cut flowers, roses and lilac and lilies. Chiles, marinara, kielbasa, chicken soup, and burgers on the grill. Clean clothes, dirty clothes, bleach, a hint of fear, damp wool, and something you could never, ever name.

patience

Kudos to the saint who has the patience of a man. Who can sit on the moist earth of springtime and explain an ant's life to a group of first-graders. Who has the poise to rein in his own free-wheeling gallop and walk beside the shuffle-stepped and lonely old man who lives three floors below. Who makes the time to walk the unfamiliar ridges of his own inner landscape. Who counts to ten or a hundred or a thousand before he acts. The patient man sounds like the oboe, clear and steady and calm. He will take as long as it takes to help his daughter learn to ride a two-wheeler. He will give as long as it takes to turn and break every last clod in the garden. As long as it takes to find the answer he had within him all along. He will perch a child on his knees for as many moments as he needs to untangle the strings of a bright yellow yo-yo. To untangle his own strings, a man must be patient. Then patience is his for all time.

Resilience
resilience

He's back! He had to hit bottom and he did, and now he's on the rebound. After he lost the business, he found a new position with one of his best customers and he's got a steady paycheck and a pension to boot. He lost everything in the flood, but he found a lot of support and now he's getting back on his feet. It's been over a year since the funeral, and now he's beginning to date. He's never been one to stay down for too long. The pneumonia took a terrible toll, but he's responding to treatment and recovering well. That whole affair with his brother was pretty devastating, but you know he's resilient, and the future looks fine. He was so far along, and out dropped the bottom, he was back to Square One in the wink of an eye. It seemed he was dribbling for quite a long time, but it's a whole new ball game, and he's bounced back just fine.

originality

Face it, there's nobody out there quite like him! Who else would do some of those crazy things he does? Who else walks like him, talks like him, does those unforgettable little things just like him? When they made him, they not only broke the mold, they scattered the pieces over the deepest part of the ocean. As a piece of work, he's priceless. You can always count on him to come up with a totally new idea for the annual fund raiser, or a never-before-tried twist for the town picnic. He says he was the first ever to start a wave at a soccer game, and you wouldn't put it past him. Who else would put a pair of socks, a leftover pan of brownies, and a new kitten together in quite that way? Who else would slice through the same-old, same-old, and dazzle us with his brand-new design? Who else never ceases to amaze us with his entirely original approach to everything? He's a one-in-a-million man, or a one-in-a-billion times ten.

Generosity

When a man starts giving, he truly starts living. He's up at the crack of dawn, flipping pancakes at the community breakfast. He's sweating in the sun, picking up broken glass and planting saplings at the new park. Rolling up his sleeve and making a fist for the neighborhood blood drive. When he gets a new sweater, he gives away the old one, even though it's barely worn. Ditto with the shoes that someone convinced him he really ought to have. Generous of spirit, he's making chocolate cake with the children at the shelter and letting everybody lick the bowl. Generous of heart, he's coaching paraplegics on the court and not cutting anybody any slack. He's digging wells in Nicaragua, delivering water and grain to Native American relocation resistors, and reattaching hands and feet for bomb victims all over the globe. Generous to a fault, he's slipping two hundred dollars to his favorite poet and slipping out the door before a word can be spoken. His generosity is its own reward.

Indecision

He wants to. No, he doesn't. It sounds good. Well, maybe not. It makes a lot of sense, but something smells fishy. *I'm torn. I'm confused. Is it God or is it Coyote?* Heads, it's a keeper. Tails, it's history. On the one hand. On the other hand. On the other. Someone's going to make a fortune and it may as well be him. *It's too risky. The stakes are too high. I can't decide. I can't make up my mind. What if I go for it and then something better comes along?* He'll do it. No, this isn't a good time. Maybe tomorrow. Maybe in the spring. He'd love to. But. He wants to. But. *A little voice says* Yes *and that old demon voice says* No. *All the reasons are there, but my heart isn't in it. They'll just have to wait till I make up my mind.* Sometimes the decision not to decide is the best decision of all. And the man who makes it isn't confused: He's simply *in decision.*

Moments

The moment they told him his father was dead. The moment he looked in the mirror and knew that his life would never again be the same. The moment the man said, *You've got the job.* The moment they said he was fired. The moment they announced the award and gave him the money. The moment he learned they were pregnant. The moment he learned they were not. The very first moment he remembers as a child. The very last moment before the sheriff came. The moment the ball hit the rim, and the moment it fell through the basket. His first moment behind the wheel of a car. His first moment in the back seat of same. That exact moment the phone rang, and he knew just who was calling. That horrible moment, in the therapist's office, when he remembered what he had tried so long to forget. Those moments he knew he was falling in love, and the moments just when he fell out. Moment by moment, the mile-long procession. Minute by minute, the moments of life.

Style
style

Don't know what to call it, but he's got it and then some. Two parts retro and a smidgen of camp, with some Wall Street thrown in for good measure. Three-fourths prep school and one-third Yankee and a hint of Milwaukee to give him pizzazz. He's Venice Beach in a three-piece suit and in-line skates; Abe Lincoln in sweats and headphones; Chattanooga with a certain charm that can only be called Chicago Chic. He's sporting muddy cowboy boots and a pocket protector filled with leaking pens—and somehow, on him, it works. His running shoes are metallic gold and his trench coat is forest green, and he's walking through the lobby like he owns the joint. He's doing lipstick and everyone loves it. Wearing a studded dog collar that nobody questions. You'll never miss him. He's the one wearing black jeans when everybody else is wearing black tie. He's decked out in diaphanous when the dress code says denim. He's asking for buttermilk when the menu says fine wines. He may look like he's out of sync and out of step, but you've got to give him credit: *The man's got style*.

Opinions

opinions

Name any subject from A to Z, and he's sure to have an opinion. He's strongly opposed or greatly in favor, and somehow he knows that he's right. He wants to tear up the highways and tear down the prisons, and is sure that our social fabric is torn past repair. He'll debate anybody anytime on anything, and he'll never cry *Uncle* until his point of view is the only one left. (Or right, as the case may be.) Radio talk shows are his favorite forum, and it's banal and boring if there's barely a fight. He's not one to hedge or to sit on a fence; his most titillating evening is when talk turns to defense! He's sure of exactly what the Brits ought to do, and he knows how the Balkans can get out of their stew. He thinks consensus is a crime against nature—and while he's on the subject, here's what's right about crime! In my humble opinion, though he's rigid as glue, I'd rather rush to hear him than some others, wouldn't you?

vulnerability

vulnerability

It's a rare and precious gift when a man exposes his innermost core. He stands naked before you, stripped of pretense. Watch his face soften and clench at the same time. Feel him tighten, then lighten as he drops layer and layer of protective armor and lets go of pounds and pounds of emotional baggage. Listen quietly. You may hear him tell you that he is frightened, that he doesn't know where to turn, that he is beset with confusion, that the wheel house of his mind is filled with a deafening clanging he can no longer deny. If asked, walk beside him as he moves hesitantly into dark and scary places he has never visited before. Honor the fact that you have been invited on the journey, and honor the moment, for it is sacred. Leave your own defenses behind, and prepare to be vulnerable too.

Playfulness

Let's go out and play! Let's get out our skates and skateboards and not come home 'til it's way past dark. We can find a really good stick and play fetch with the dog. Let me show you how to do a really great cannonball off the diving board! Last one in the water is a rotten egg! Knock, knock, who's there? Guess what? That's what! What an awesome day to fly kites! Let's do tag and you be it! No, I wanna play statues! Meet you by the courts and we can all play Horse! Nobody's here! Let's take over the monkey bars! Can you jump off the swing without breaking your arm? SNOWBALL FIGHT! I'll get my bike and we can pretend we're riding horses. Grab your brother's football and we'll toss it around. Let's play triple solitaire! The loser gets to play 156-card pickup! Even better, let's toss the cards into your grandpa's hat! Let's play volleyball! Who needs a net? Come on! Let's run through the sprinklers and throw water balloons from the third-floor balcony. Dinner time already? But we've barely started to play...

Calm
calm

Sometimes a man walks into the eye of a raging storm, and suddenly all is quiet. With a well-chosen word or a well-focused gaze, he ushers in a peacefulness that is felt by all around him. Perhaps a word is not even necessary, and by the simple fact of his being there, a hush settles in like a new-fallen blanket of snow. Fears are quelled and voices quieted. Questions are answered, and quarreling put to rest. Tranquillity reigns. When he carries his own calmness within him, a man radiates calm in every direction. He need not announce *I am in charge* or wrest control from others. He need not bark orders or fly into a flurry of efficiency. His very breathing soothes; the unruffled rhythm of his movement lulls the air itself into a calming peace. He takes nothing and gives nothing but calm. And when he must leave, the calm lingers on.

Arms
arms

Yes! to the right to bare arms. Sunned and weathered arms, farm arms, hot and spicy arms swaying to a Latin beat. Arms presented in tank tops and muscle shirts and short-cropped T-shirts with the sleeves ripped off. Arms offered before crossing the street or stepping off the ladder and onto the roof. Arms that lightly brush up against us on the bus and double-wrap around us as we sleep. Biceps lifting boxes, solving equations on the chalkboard, directing traffic the day the power blew. Arms scarred from the fire, frail and weakened arms that silently ask to be steadied so he can write his name. Talking arms speaking in sign language, moving like magic and breathing life into words we can see. Freckled arms, speckled arms, saluting smartly as the ship pulls slowly away. Arms! Lifting little ones out of harm's way, reaching up to pluck the topmost grapes from the arbor. Raised in fierce defiance, raised in Olympic triumph, linked in unity and raised in praise, we are charmed and disarmed by his arms.

prayers

Oh Dear God, help me to be the man you would have me be—a loving father, husband, partner, friend. Goddess Divine, show me the way to honor your earthly body, your sacred rivers, fields and forests, and to embrace all your children, two-legged and four-, as my brothers and sisters. O Great Spirit, let me recognize that you are everywhere, and that your presence in my life transcends anything I ever could imagine. Sweet Jesus, wash me clean of my sins of arrogance and pride, and guide me to live a life of love. Please, Lord, help me transform my anger and frustration into forgiveness and compassion for myself and others. I pray for the understanding that there is something larger and infinitely more powerful than myself, and for the strength to surrender and release my need to analyze, to figure out, and to control the people, situations, and conditions around me. Help me to see in new ways, to hear that which lies beneath yet is never spoken, and to create only that which serves the highest good. Let it be. Amen. So it is.

Fight

Some things are worth fighting for, and sometimes we need a good man to help fight the good fight. He needs to stop shadow boxing and go a few rounds with a worthy opponent. He can duel with ideas and wage war with his words. He can joust for just causes and rise up over outrage and object to objectionable actions. When a warrior speaks for peace, his voice can be the shot heard 'round the world. A man needs enough fight in him to do battle over bureaucratic blunders and go hand-to-hand for human rights. Who's going to fight for freedom if a man has all the fight knocked out of him? Who's going to wrestle with oppression, if a man is convinced that the wars are all won? Sometimes resisting is the path of least resistance. If a man saves his fight for all the right reasons, his fight will well serve when he's called on to fight.

Buddies

Love a man, love his buddies. The one he's known since childhood, who never left him hanging, who bailed him out of jail that night. That whole gang from college who got a little out of hand at the wedding, then chipped in to pay your first month's rent and the security deposit, too. That crazy old guy, the one with the thick accent, who you don't hear from for years, and suddenly he's at the door with homemade yogurt and a jar of garlic olives he picked and cured himself. The threesome he's golfed with every month for thirteen years. His pool-playing partner. His buddies from the war. The truckers he'll never meet, who stayed with him on the CB radio and talked him through that nasty storm over Donner Pass. That young blind man he plays bluegrass banjo with, who came and stayed with you when he was out of town and you got the call about your Dad. They may make you crazy and you won't always like them, but if you truly love a man, you're bound to love his buds.

Moods
moods

He's up, he's down, he's all around. He's talking a blue streak; his is the silence before the storm. He's high on life and the sky's the limit and nothing's gonna stop him now. He puts on Chaka Khan and starts cleaning out the closets at 6 A.M., and he's still going strong at midnight. He's in one of those moods. He swears he'll never shave or take a shower again. He's not answering the phone and wouldn't want to talk to anyone if he did. He's frustrated and impatient and he's been that way all week. He's just in one of those moods. He's giddy and playful and wants to play hooky from work and go sailing instead. He's all wrapped up with the one he loves, and the thought of letting go makes him crazy. He doesn't want to get out of bed. Wants to make love all day long. Wants to be naked outdoors. Oh yeah, it's one of *those* moods. It's nothing too serious, no diagnosis needed. It's just that he's moving through moods.

Skin
skin

It matters not much what skin a man's in. It can be thick as the hide of a bull, or thin and sheer as a gossamer wing. It can gleam with a darkness black as coal, or fade into the sunlight with a translucent pale, or enthrall us with colors no artist could ever concoct. What paint chip could copy his café au lait? Or capture the bloom of his ruddy, red glow? A man's skin lies smooth and taut, hangs loose and dimpled, stretches over muscles and bone and gathers in valleys and canyons and rests atop ridges. Touch the stories only his skin can tell. The still-tender scars from the helicopter crash, from the New Year's Day fire, from the transplanted heart. Over here are fields of freckles, skin aft and fore, and a patch as soft as a baby's behind. This is skin to sink into. Skin to stroke slowly. Skin is a bag for carrying bones, until like a rebirthing rattler, he slips out of his skin.

Aggression

Listen to me and listen up good! In the right quantity, at the right time, and aimed in the right direction, aggression is one powerful tool. Sometimes a man needs to pump a little adrenaline to get the big job done. He needs to move some energy and make things happen so everybody wins. There comes that moment when the kid gloves come off and the work gloves go on! *Are you hearing what I'm saying?* The man who wants to go boldly where no man has gone before had better light a few fires first. If necessary, he's got to slam the system into high gear and knock away any debris that's standing in the way. Sometimes a man has to kick some proverbial butt to move the pendulum off dead center and get it swinging toward ultimate balance. When you want to move a mountain or revolutionize an industry or transform a planet, you need a man who can handle the high-octane fuel of aggression. *You better be listening, 'cause I'm not going to repeat myself!*

flexibility

He never said he would never say never, and chances are he won't. He'll bend over backwards when an outcome is critical, but he won't bend in the other direction. He's a blue-ribbon negotiator, because he knows how to give a little give-and-take. Casting words in stone may have worked for Moses, but it's not his style. He's up every day at 5 A.M. for yoga, and he can still shimmy around the corner in the crawl space with a pail of water in his hand. He's a strict vegetarian, but when he stayed at the home of some folks who had nothing to give but a steaming bowl of mutton stew, he accepted their humble offerings with relish. He once swore he would never, ever get married, but he's reconsidering. Ditto for divorce. He said it would be a cold day in hell before he would drive cross-country with the family again, but that was way before the mini-van. He's got one hard-and-fast rule that he'll never go soft on: Pig-headedness may work just fine for a pig, but it doesn't do much for a man.

Clarity

He's as crystal clear as a high mountain lake on a crisp autumn day. Yes! He's selling his car and getting a bike. No! He won't accept the offer to run the Singapore operation. Absolutely! He'll enter the marathon to help raise money for AIDS research. Thanks but no thanks, he'd rather spend the holidays with his stepchildren. A three-month hike along the Appalachian Trail? You bet. Pick up stakes and follow his partner across the country? In a heartbeat. His decisiveness defines his destiny. His depth of understanding declares his direction. He's calling his brother to apologize after twenty-five years. Finally getting what they meant when they said *You don't get it!* Slipping a ring on the finger of his lifelong lover. Choosing to thrive and not merely survive; trading in the same-old, same-old, for the what's-new, what's-now. He cuts through confusion with the precision of a finely-honed saber. He's so certain, we're certain he's clear.

Neckwear

His neck need not necessarily be naked! Not when he can wear Windsor-knotted silk ties or polka-dotted bow ties. Not when he can cravat! What better place than a man's neck for hanging sunglasses on a string, a quartz crystal on a golden chain, or a Celtic talisman on a leather cord? Look what he's wearing today! Unwrap the scarf his ex-mother-in-law crocheted, and you'll find last night's hickey trying to hide 'neath a turtle, while his eldest son's dog tags lie next to his heart. Not to mention an albatross (or two), and a bright red swath of razor rash. One day, he's Southern formal in nothing but a Colonel's tie and a bucket of fried chicken under his arm. Next day he's doing the Virginia Reel with a red bandanna neckerchief, and grooving to Hendrix in a macramé choker. We love when a man wears next to nothing, as long as his neck is done up in style.

Strength
strength

A man always struggles with the idea of strength. Is he too strong, not strong enough? We see him holding up under the weight of a world that demands he is always strong. That he is the strong man at the circus, Arnold Schwarzenegger, Superman, and Hercules rolled into one. Watch him go to work, day after day, to a place where he is beaten down or beaten up and comes home beaten to a pulp. Someone has told him, over and over, that his job is, first, to be strong. Is he strong enough to be vulnerable, to say *I can't, I never could, I'm awfully tired of trying?* Is he strong enough to lift himself up, to lift others up and raise them to the sky? The troubled, young man he met at church. The woman in the lab who came in Thursday bruised at the hands of a weak man who thought he was strong. They are touched, we are touched, by a man who knows his own strength and wields it well.

green thumb

He's never more at home than when he's in the garden. He kneels in the dirt and talks to the sprouts, and his roses are blue-ribbon winners. He plants by the light of the moon and weeds before the sun is high, and treats his tomatoes to Mozart. He tosses seeds into a rock-strewn plot of land, speaks a few words to a cloudless sky, and the next thing you know, he's got eggplant. While others are battling beetles, he's arranging marigolds and making tarragon vinegar and pleasing big crowds with his pesto. His Boston Fern has been with him since Harvard, and his Philodendron dates back to Philly. He finds orphaned house plants in alley trash cans, and nurses them back to fruition. No self-respecting butterfly would miss his bee balm, and the deer come around to admire, not gnaw. His rooftop garden is an earthly oasis, and the grass on his side is decidedly greener.

Instinct

Face it! Man is an animal! A living, breathing beast who just happened to step on a fast track to civilization and had a hard time getting off the treadmill. His instinct says to Hunt! Protect! Breed! Prey! Fight! Sleep! Mark Territory! Die! It is a man's nature to defend the pride, to bring home the wildebeest, to mate for life or mate to create life. He's hard-wired to jump if attacked, lash out if provoked, pounce to protect his offspring, and to preen and pose as much as he wants to attract the object of his desires. He eats with his hands and licks his plate clean, spends hours picking nits off himself and others, and crawls into his cave when the sun goes down. If you have trouble with that, try teaching your Rottweiler to eat with a fork.

Sweetness

How sweet he is! He sent flowers from halfway around the world, just to say *Aloha*. He was on the phone for hours, finding the perfect hideaway lodge for the perfect getaway. He called ahead, then sent a sweet note afterwards. Remembered your mother's best friend's birthday. Gave you the last two bites of his favorite dessert and offered to go out in the middle of the night to get more. No wonder he attracts people like bees to a hive! He's sugar-coated, dipped in honey, drizzled with chocolate and delicious through and through! After your surgery, he made you chicken soup and cornbread. For no reason at all, on that bright sunny Sunday, he served you breakfast in bed, right down to the red rose in the bud vase. He played tiddly winks and leapfrog with the kids for hours, so you could visit with your oldest, dearest friend. Every time you turn around, he's whispering sweet nothings and sweet everythings and sweet somethings-in-between. He may have a hard candy shell, but once you hit that soft, creamy filling, you can swoon in the syrup of his sweetness.

Dexterity

Jack, be nimble! Watch him juggle seventeen balls in the air and put out fast-spreading forest fires and download in six languages all at the same time, without ever leaving his tiny office cubicle. Isn't he the one who once addressed holiday cards with his right hand while sewing on buttons with his left, and pumping up an inner tube with his foot? Even with his prosthesis, who would have thought he could play the harp? His hands are quicker than everyone's eyes, and no one can figure out his coin tricks. He's got all the edge pieces firmly in place, while the others are still unpacking the puzzle. Thanks to his teeth, he always gets the knots out. Always finds the splinter. Has no problem at all checking his messages, sending his email, programming his pager, and recalculating his mortgage payments, all while he's trimming the hedges. When it comes to splitting hairs, he's supremely adroit and, admittedly, he's ambidextrous.

Balance

He's a master of equilibrium. He makes equal time and space for his body, mind, and spirit. He'll make all the right phone calls and send all the right letters—then he'll fall to his knees and quietly pray. He reads *The Wall Street Journal* before breakfast, and the *Kama Sutra* before bed. He'll design an incredibly complex website—and then wind down with a few hundred hands of computer solitaire. He's entranced by the blending of science and spirit; he trusts his intuition as he trusts his PC. He believes that laughter is the best medicine, and after weighing his options, he'll take a course of antibiotics, too. He'll work overtime when things get hectic, and take off early when things are slow. He keeps cool and calm while drama rages around him, and does his best to avoid too-high highs and too-low lows. He's climbing the ladder, but it's a walk, not a race. Once a man finds himself in a true state of balance, he'll push a wheelbarrow on a tightrope with impeccable grace.

Hands

How the hands of a man come in handy! Long and tapered fingers wriggling into and out of tight places. Strong and stubby hands kneading knots out of necks. The rough, callused, dirt-stained palms of a man who works with his hands every day; the cuticle-free and clear-polished hands of a man who gets a manicure every week. Sweet and sweaty palms, nervous hands shaking just when he wishes they wouldn't, and holding firm precisely when he prays they would. *What is the sound of one hand clapping?* These are the hands that gently stroke the baby's cheek, that fly over the rows and rows of keys on the antique organ, that twist off the lids of defiant jars of pickles and salad dressing. These are the fingers that hook unreachable eyes and fasten delicate gold chains behind necks, and later that same day reach right in and pull the wayward bone out of the neighbor's dog's throat. Hands that we hold, limp wrists that fold, *Oooh! Not there, your hands are so cold!* He lost his hands in Nam and now his hands are metal, and he ties ponytail ribbons like a pro. When a man asks *Can I give you a hand?* answer *Yes, but I might not return it.*

Wisdom

When a man attains a certain age, he can be anointed with the wisdom of the ages. But not a moment before. Wisdom is not learned in a book, and while the young may receive a sage's wisdom, they may not understand it for years to come. When a man has conquered fear and foolishness, he will find the joy in wisdom. When his intelligence is tempered with a wealth of experience, he will find the wisdom within. He will cut through clutter with a well-honed mind. He will see the light of truth shining in the darkness; he will see the essential answer at the heart of the quest. This is the wise grandfather, listening intently, silently thinking, and dispensing his knowledge with wit and with wisdom. He has worked a lifetime, raised his family, set out on his journey, and found his way home. What he has to share is as timeless as Solomon, so seek out his wisdom whenever you can. Choosing to do otherwise shows no wisdom at all.

touch

Oh, for the touchable touch of a man! Foot rubs and neck rubs and rub-a-dub-dub-rubs in the tub. The way he touched your arm in court, and you suddenly knew that everything would be all right. The light touch of his index finger drawing an undulating line from the tip of your nose to the tip of your toes. How well he speaks the language of touch! How his comforting hand on the shoulder says *I'm right here beside you*; how the back of his hand grazing your cheek says *I know it's been hard*. Arresting caresses and fingers that linger, and fondling you're so very fond of. That next-to-nothing touch in the magical spot that stops the baby's hiccups every time. The touching way he brushes the hair out of his younger brother's eyes, even though they're both in their eighties. His insatiable desire to touch every rock and every tree he passes. That personal touch that goes into everything he does. We see how he touches everyone around him, and how could we help but be touched?

Wants

What a man wants is what every human wants. To be totally accepted and never taken for granted. To be celebrated for the rare and precious treasure that he is. To be understood—*really understood*—by at least one other person on Earth (and preferably by a few more). To experience rapturous, unconditional love and to offer the same in return, without hesitation. Oh, simply to be wanted! To have someone, *anyone!*, care where he is and whether he'll be home. To have someone, *anyone!*, to call when he's scared, he's alone, he's beside himself with joy or beneath himself with despair. What does a man want? To need and be needed, to be interdependent and never again co-dependent. He yearns to work at what matters, to give freely of his gifts, to pass along something of unquestionable value to another, who can pass it along again. To remember who he is and why he's here, and who passed this way before him. Forget all that talk about sports cars and sailboats. A man wants the things that money can't buy.

Camaraderie

camaraderie

Yo, Bro! We love the way a man loves his buddies. All bear hugs and noogies on the upper arm and *Hit me as hard as you can!* on the belly, and just-right, light slaps from behind. Locker room stories and barracks stories and duck-blind tales in whispered voices. The ones that got away. The ones they wish they had never let go. Men stay awake half the night playing cards, and then get up before dawn to steal away to the cabin and fish. They jump on their bikes and leap in their jeeps and take off like young stags on holiday. Watch them come to the aid of their own! Forty years later, they're still twelve years old, down by the quarry, pledging themselves as blood brothers while the whole town looks for them like crazy. Beneath-the-skin brothers, they high-five and thumbs-up and pump the air wildly and raise a toast high for the spirit and flesh of the corps.

Eccentricity

Who wants a man who's ordinary, anyway? Give us the oddball and unorthodox, the wayward and rare, the man who was conspicuously absent from the convention hall when conventional wisdom was born. What a breath of fresh air is a man who wears his shoes on his head! What a total turn-on is a man who turns to Chaucer when everyone else is turning on MTV! If a man would rather hang out with a fish than a *fraulein*, who are we to declare him off-center? Stop fooling yourself. You know you're not the only one who deeply loved *The Nutty Professor*. You know you were green with envy that Morticia got Gomez, and you got Gomer. You know you've got a side that's a little bit kinky! So why not hook up with a certified kook? There's a spark in a man who's truly eccentric, and it's exceptionally, exceedingly lovable.

Unmentionables

Oh, let's mention them anyway! Ballooning boxers that hide everything behind rows of Irish Setters and Model A Fords and dancing walleye pike. Hiked up, pulled up, yanked up, falling down, waistbands desperately seeking waist or lying taut and trim against ultimate abs. Briefly mentioned, the briefest of satin bikinis, iridescent colors of a peacock, leaving nothing whatsoever to the imagination and absolutely everything to fate. Tartan flannels and white stretchies and athletic grays hung over doorknobs and slung across the room and rolled into balls, hiding for who knows how long in lockers and laundry baskets. *(Okay, you're right, I promised never to mention the underwear-on-the-head-dance.)* It's a two-point, sling-shot hook shot into the hamper…and the crowd goes wild! Long-legged thermals for slipping into before stepping onto snowshoes. Not to mention, of course, those dry-clean-only silk thongs for slipping into and out of before (or after) anything at all.

Grace
grace

Let us give thanks for grace in a man. We are taken by a body that moves in grace, that dances *Swan Lake*, sprints for a touchdown, or sutures a face with remarkable grace. We watch him stacking boxes with graceful precision and sweeping the floors with impeccable grace. His legs may be lifeless, yet his arms move with the flutter and flow of birds in flight. He is the quintessential gracious host. His home is warm and welcoming, and his table is set with linen and china, with flowers artfully arranged and food lovingly prepared. Goodness gracious, it's all so inviting, we never want to leave! His grace runs deep and rises to the top under pressure. He knows just when to offer the perfect word, just when to put out his comforting hand, just when to silently retreat and fade graciously into the background. When he is in a state of grace, we are grateful, for we are there, too. For the grace in a man, say Amen.

Shoulders

Shouldn't something be said about shoulders? Broad shoulders with room enough to lean on and cry on and sit on to see above the crowd. Shoulders that carry sleepy toddlers up the stairs, and fifty-pound backpacks down into the canyon. Shoulders bent and a bit droopy from trying to carry the weight of the world, because someone once told him he should. Because someone once told him a man shouldn't lean on anybody. Because someone once told him a man should be strong enough to support his family. It's what a man should be, they said. Shoulders locked in place from too many *shoulds*. Shoulders sore from sitting hunched over too long in front of a computer. Shoulders tight and tense from too many hours putting shoulder to the wheel and nose to the grindstone. Shoulders that freeze and pull the first time he decides he really should get out and play tennis. Really should pump iron for a while. Really should spread his wings and fly. We wrap our arms around shoulders and hang sports jackets on shoulders and stand shoulder-to-shoulder when the going gets tough. Shouldn't something be said about shoulders?

Daydreams

Dreams that won't fit into a man's night, spill out into his days. While the professor drones on about the fall of the Iron Curtain, he is passing through a land of golden trees. He rides a paint horse and stops to play the flute along the way. He disrobes and is about to step into a magnificent pool of sparkling clear water, when the professor bellows his name for the fifth time. He is working the line, and his hands remain focused while his mind starts to wander. He is twelve years old again and he is running from his father, running to his secret place behind the junkyard. He's tossing perfect pitches against an old wooden fence, one after another. He is young and invincible and can do no wrong— and then his supervisor's voice yanks him back to reality. He is pushing his youngster on a swing, and he envisions getting that promotion and getting that raise and getting the recognition he's deserved for so long. He feels the tug of a little hand on his pants leg, and the dream dissolves into the day.

Courage

What, then, is the courage befitting a man? A man's true courage rises from his heart and infuses his spirit. It strengthens him to fight for what matters, or to choose not to fight. To be the fifth of his line who attends the academy, or to be the first in the family who will not go. One kind of courage leaves his warm bed and cries out *Who goes there?* in the darkened night. Another peers into his darkened soul and poses the question *Who lives here?* Courage can be quiet. Courage can be still. A courageous man walks into the Vet Center and announces *This is a cry for help*, and lets another man hold him close while he cries. He pours his feelings onto paper and then reads his poems out loud to a roomful of strangers. Dances across stage in his wheelchair. Puts down the bottle for the last time. What courage has a man who will tear away the chains that have held him for so long and find the freedom to loudly proclaim *Here I am!* A man is justly honored when we recognize the courageous acts he has met in life, and not just the courage he may meet at death's door.

Flamboyance

Flash it, boyfriend! Shake your bootie and shake up the whole place with a wave of your white-gloved hand. Make a drop-dead entrance and drag it out and nonchalantly ask, *Who, moi?* Go ahead and make 'em wait. Make 'em wait real long. Make a scene that will make 'em forget they ever knew Michael Jackson existed. Go all out and be the prince of flamboyance. Wear a lot of gold jewelry all at once and be certain that everyone sees it. Flash a wad of bills just for show; then flash a few more just to show that you mean it. Show up at Mardi Gras and show 'em something they haven't seen since Liberace. Wear hot pink in the coolest places. Honor the memory of Elvis and create a little Graceland all your own. Go baroque unless you're broke, and then you can go rococo. Draw attention to yourself and then revel in being the center of attention. If you're thinking of going Gothic, go back to your dressing room and think again, okay? Every boy can use a bit of flamboyance—and when he grows to a man, he can use a bit more.

Intuition

Something told him to get off the plane, so he was on his way to Dallas while everybody else sat on the runway for a five-hour delay. He just had a feeling, so he checked up on Grandma and found she had fallen by the back stairs. He never got the phone message, but his sixth sense told him to pick up a chicken on the way home anyway. For some unknown reason, he walked the long way, and ran into his long-lost theater buddy after seventeen years. The odometer said 24,530, and he played the number and won sixty bucks. He had this crazy hunch that hemp was happening, and laughed all the way to the bank. His broker said *Buy!* and his intuition said *Sell!*, and now he gives out stock tips for five hundred bucks a pop. Totally out of the blue, he wondered how she was doing, and ten minutes later, her email arrived. His gut told him that something didn't quite fit, and *Hoo Boy!* was he glad that he listened. He's heard about women's intuition, but for some reason he can't quite explain, he's inclined to think it's a crock.

self-reliance

He declared his own independence when he was just fifteen, and he's been a self-made man ever since. He figures he's got two strong legs and two healthy feet, so he might as well stand on them. He's his own boss and his own best friend—and he bakes his own sourdough bread in a wood burning stove he fires up every morning. He rides his bicycle everywhere he goes, grows his own greens in his hydroponic greenhouse, and heats his handmade hogan with the power of the sun. Darn! He even mends his own socks! He can put out an alert on short-wave radio in case the phones go down, and he's not about to run out of toilet paper in the middle of a storm. For him, the 'Net is for bringing home the brown trout—and not for idle chit-chat. He'll carry his canoe on his back to reach uncharted waters, and suck out his own snake bite as long as he can reach. If he can't be his own man first of all, then whose could he possibly be?

t-shirts

A T-shirt fits a man to a T. Plastered tight across his chest or pulled down over his bulging belly. Virginal white and bleached to perfection, or stained and smeared with mystery sludge. Equally tantalizing on Teamsters or teachers, on ministers, mailmen, and major league stars. Tiny or tent-like, they show up at truck stops or under tuxedos, or tied around heads. Pulled up high to reveal sweaty torsos, or hung over posts while the digging gets done. T-shirts make fashion statements in bright and bold colors, with sleeves rolled up or torn off with teeth. They turn men into walking billboards for statements of every hue and cry, demanding an end to gun control and calling for an end to uncontrolled logging and proclaiming that Jesus is coming, and soon. T-shirts brag that the wearer was at concerts never attended, cities never visited, trendy cafes never set foot in, and marathons certainly never run. Remove your shirt sir, if you please! Tie-dyed or tailored, T's are a tease.

Foolhardiness

There he is, like the fool of olde, boyishly grinning with one foot dangling over the edge of the mountaintop. Getting up from his desk to shoot hoops with the teenagers and forgetting quite how long it's been since his knee has rotated in so many directions at once. Inventing the perfect accessory for a product that became defunct just a month ago. Scrambling up hills in his street shoes and thin black socks, leaning over a little too far, jumping in where it's a little too rocky, eyes shining with the memory of that summer in '68 when he was invincible and in love and the world was a cauldron of youthful exuberance. Oh, there he goes again! Spending the retirement fund on a motorcycle, shiny and red and oh, yeah, open to the sky! Tearing out the closet shelves and promising to have it all done by Sunday at 6:00, without fail. Dancing for joy on the spur of the moment, he is wonderfully, terribly, foolishly foolish.

Devotion
devotion

Not that slavish or guilt-driven devotion of old, but the real, true thing. He nursed his Dad through his last dying days, and he did it out of heartfelt devotion. He still calls his Mother and joins her for tea, and if you ask why, it's devotion. When it comes to his children or his sweetheart, there ain't no mountain high enough or river wide enough to keep him away. He's fiercely loyal to the people he works with and it isn't because of the paycheck he pulls. His grandfather dedicated his life to social justice, and now he's dedicated to doing the same. He's committed to doing all he can do to end hunger in his lifetime. He's devoted to living a life simply devoted to love. He may not be the world's most devout churchgoer, but he religiously dedicates time every day to replenish his spirit and awaken his soul. When it comes to saving whales, he admits he's a zealot. He'll do whatever it takes to champion his cause. And the cause of all that is devotion.

Tongue

Hail the humble lingua! Without it, we could never watch a man do all those entertaining things with an ice cream cone. We would never feel his agony as he stands tongue-tied and speechless at the podium, or share the joke of his tongue-in-cheek story. He lazily licks an all-day sucker for an entire week, and never passes up the chance to lick his plate clean at the finest restaurant. He rolls his Rs like he was born and raised in Buenos Aires. He can say Red Leather Yellow Leather faster and longer than anyone in town. He charms the committee with his silver-tongued rhetoric, and test-drives the salt lick before leaving the feed store. He licks his lips when he thinks nobody is looking, and touches his tongue to the tip of his nose when he hopes that they are. When he's with the old ones, he'll slip into the mother tongue and before you know it, everyone is weeping and pining for home. He remembers the day he stuck his tongue out at the Mother Superior, and oh, what a tongue-lashing she gave! There's much more to say on the tip of his tongue, but I don't want to start tongues a-wagging.

Whisperings

The bigger the man, the more we're entranced when he whispers. He nestles his mouth right next to our ears, and before he utters a syllable, we feel his warm breath and a hint of whisker. His quiet words fill our inner ears: *I love you so much. Don't turn around, but guess who just walked in on the arm of guess-who? I need a bathroom now.* After a parade of pontificating, podium-pounding windbags, he steps up to the microphone and begins to whisper. Everyone strains to hear, edging forward in their chairs. His barely audible words carry unspeakable weight, immeasurable power. He whispers a last message to Poppa, never knowing if the old man understands any of it. He whispers to himself in the mirror, quiet words of confidence and perhaps a hint of prayer. We've seen him whisper to the weed trimmer after seven unsuccessful starts. We watch him whisper to the pitcher at the bottom of the ninth, with bases loaded. We see him kneel beside the tiny headstones, and we wonder what he whispers. His words can carry a wallop, when they're barely a wisp of a whisper.

power

He's got the power! He's plugged into a new source of personal power and he's finding new ways to light up his world. He's learned a powerful lesson: Once a man steps into his circle of power, he need never pull power from another again. He knows that true power-lifting is using his power to lift people up, and never to keep anyone down. It's the power that empowers others to find their way, to discover their own place of power. The pure, potent power of a man is measured in the lives he inspires and the hearts he activates and the right actions he generates. It's a powerful man who stands in his convictions and moves with courage and carries his weight. When a man believes that his power resides in his bankbook or sits in his garage or in his job title, he's seeking a false sense of power. When he seeks the power that resides within, then a man is a true powerhouse.

Artistry
artistry

Oh, what a piece of work is man when he puts his hands to a work of art! He tends the downtown gardens with a flair for color, shadow, and sun. The yard is dotted with his birdhouses of uncommon design, rendered in form that would make Frank Lloyd write home. For the fiftieth anniversary party, he painstakingly painted a street map of Charleston on the sugary top of a cake. The symmetry in his sock drawer has made others swoon! Look at the mosaics he tiled into the kitchen counter. See the lamps he made from scraps of copper tubing and oversized sheets of mulberry paper. He cuts hair like a master; his flan is first-rate; his penmanship rivals the script of a scribe. His shoes are so shiny you can see an angel's reflection. See how artistically he's hung the family photos? How skillfully he repairs the hole in the rug? He's humble and shy when you call him an artist, but so much that he does is what we call fine art.

Clothes

He's dashing and debonair in an Italian suit and a flamboyant silk scarf loosely tossed over his shoulder. He's down-home and dusty in dungarees and steel-tipped boots and a faded blue workshirt aged like fine French wine. He's all decked out in his dress uniform, spotless and pressed to within an inch of its life and fitting like he was born to wear it. *Who would have thought that bib overalls from the big man's store could look so fine!* He's dreamy in the plush terry robe that accidentally found its way into his bag at the hotel (and accidentally falls open every time he moves). His red suspenders and candy-striped bow tie are the picture of fashion perfection. He's jumping on his bike in leggings with just a hint of nylon, flying to Philly in his bomber jacket and aviator glasses, and kilting up for a parade at noon. *Uh-oh, he's doing bermudas and sandals with socks again!* Nattily dapper, he's tweeded and toppered. Terminally trendy, he's head to toe in hemp. His shirts are for polo. *Oh yes! It's a bolo!* If a man must be covered, let him do it with clothes!

Reverence

reverence

Hush, don't say a word. Let him revel in his reverence. Watch him catch the frightened spider in his hand and take it outside to a sunny patch of green. See how he stops traffic to lift the lifeless cat out of the path of untold dishonor. Shhh, do not disturb. He is deep in Ravel, lost in reverie and finding a piece of the unending universe in every note. He is staring dumbstruck at a shimmering sky and being brought to his knees in powerless surrender. Let him be. He sits in the service and weeps at the vastness of creation and the sheer wonder of it all. Nothing has prepared him for the miracle of birth, for the way his brain cannot wrap around what he has just seen and for the unimagined bewilderment that leaves him shaking and silenced with awe. He is stopped in his tracks when the hearse drives by, when the flag is lowered, when he hears a story of intolerable pain. He honors each moment as sacred, each being as worthy. Be still and regard him with reverence.

Chivalry
chivalry

Who says chivalry is dead? There's something most definitely alive in a man who's at home with manners. Who can disparage the elegant doff of a hat? Or the kind-natured kiss of a lady's hand? The courtesies of a gentlemen are always in style. He opens doors for women pushing strollers, for couriers piled high with packages, for toddlers with puppies in tow. He opens car doors without a second thought; he intends to be polite and not at all political. He would never consider coughing at the opera, smoking in the lobby, or burping in the boudoir. In a moment of chivalry, he drapes his jacket over shivering shoulders and gives up his rubbers for muddy-street feet. The chivalrous man shudders to think of sneaking two extra items through the express checkout lane. And as for the discourteous rogue who rips out the page with the crossword puzzle solution, he would challenge him to twenty paces with pistols.

Jokes

He's got a million of 'em! The one about the rabbi, the priest, and the minister. The one about the guy who got to St. Peter's pearly gates. All the ones about guys going into bars with talking animals of every kind. Puns upon puns upon puns! That gross one that we hate and told him so, and he swore he would never tell it again but he did. The ones about sex in the White House and sex in the fraternity house and sex in the House of Representatives. *Who makes these up anyway?* That whole slew of jokes about daughters: the farmer's daughter, the miller's daughter, the boss's daughter. Those really vulgar ones that crack everybody up every time. Those others that never did and never will. The one where he never gets to the punch line because he's laughing hysterically. The one where he starts over three times because he can't remember the words. He wants us to laugh, that trickster, that jester. Wants to say *Gotcha!* just one more time.

Satisfaction

He's a satisfied man, and it's written all over his face. He knows he's not done yet, but for this moment, he's satisfied with where he is. He's worked a long time and he's struggled a bit, and he feels satisfied that he's earned it. So what if he sometimes looks like the cat who swallowed the canary? He went after it and he's flush with success! Ask him how he's doing, and he'll answer *No complaints* and mean it. He feels good about how he's living his life, and he's got better things to do than to gripe. He's content with where he lives, and who he lives with, and what he contributes each day. Of course, he's still searching and finding new answers, but it's a pleasure to him to keep at it. He's satisfied knowing that it all can be better, and he's satisfied knowing he's doing his best.

Tears

Who first planted the idea that *Real men don't cry?* They tense and tighten every muscle, hundred-weight pounds of pressure to prevent the escape of that first tear, while the rest of us wait and root for the get-away water. Men's tears slip out when they most expect them and never expect them at all: in the office men's room, pink slip in hand; at the movie where the guy and his Dad reunite after thirty years; on the assembly line for who knows what reason; when his daughter stands up in front of them all and smiles and spells and speaks her mind. When his son does the right thing. Men's tears are crying to touch the light of day, to spill out onto the telephone when he gets the call that his brother is gone, that his old buddy slipped away in the night. They gather in the corners of his eyes and seep out slowly when he holds his first-born, one and only in his arms. Salty tears! It's a wonder they haven't crystallized after all these years, crashing and breaking instead of slipping, sliding, gently rolling tears.

Rituals

Every year they do it, and have for as many decades as he can remember. Rain or shine, sickness or health. They pick up a cheap bottle of wine and toast the Old Man and curse him and bless him. They drive to the Nation's Capital to leave homemade Valentines and pictures at the foot of the Wall, and to run their fingers over the names of the fathers they never met. At the Summer Solstice, he takes a young man—his own son or someone else's—far into the woods and teaches him how to find his own food and his own way and his own soul. Every year they roast chestnuts over the first fire of winter and read a poem or a story that has touched one of them deeply. Like clockwork, they meet at the shore when the blueberries are peaking, and make cobbler and jelly and jam. When he moves into a new home, before he unpacks a single box, he gathers stones and creates a medicine wheel and a quiet place to pray. Every Wednesday, he buys flowers from the red-haired woman in front of the courthouse. Roses, if she has them; daffodils, if she doesn't. He gives her a twenty, tells her to keep the change, and gives the flowers away to the first old man he sees. He does it every Wednesday, and has for as many decades as he can remember.

Willingness

willingness

He's not at all certain about this African drumming class, but he's willing to check it out. Okay, he'll give the Mex-Thai restaurant a shot. He'll meet your sister's administrative assistant for a quick microbrew, even though he's not expecting sparks to fly. A men's group? He's mighty skeptical, but he'll call the facilitator and leave a message. Leave the city and fix up an old farm? Unlikely, but he'll drive out on the weekend and poke around. He's not holding out much hope for front-row seats, but he'll get up at 3 A.M. for a good spot in line. Can't see much good in marriage counseling, but he'll go over and meet the therapist. Firmly believes that the blizzard report is nonsense, but he's willing to stock up on some extra canned goods. Absolutely refuses to vacation in Iowa, but, yeah, he'll do the virtual tour on the Internet. He's never believed that hypnosis is anything but hoo-hah, but he'll consider it if you think it will help. At least you can't say he's not willing.

Love

Man is a tireless lover! He'll love with all his heart and all his soul, and then he'll love yet more. He'll whirl and twirl in a frenzy of love, and fling open the doors and throw away the keys and toss himself on the landscape of love. He loves his brother as he loves himself. Loves his neighbor and loves each child as though it were his own. He knows the warmth of platonic love, the red-hot flush of love's desire, and the innocent glow of first, young love. He has been in the presence of love with perfect strangers, and found love wanting in the presence of friends. He keeps looking for love in all the wrong places, and when he can't be with the one he loves, he'll love the one he's with. He has been besotted with love and sweetened by love and been a suffering fool for love, and loved love all the while. It was love at first sight, it was love everlasting, it was uncommon love, and alas, all is gone. In his beloved he has found his true love, and he's brightened and lightened and frightened by love.

Words

What words can come out of the mouth of man! Fighting words that punch the air like a cannon and draw lines in the sand and give others something to push hard against. Words from the heart, sweet and tender, spoken in hushed tones and into receptive ears. Words of inspiration, brought down from on high and sent right back in the uplifted hearts of those who embrace them. Poetry and prose and lyric and lore. Limericks and letters, *Oh yes, give us more!* We see men's words etched into the marble of monuments and sprayed onto the underside of bridges and scratched into bathroom walls. They ring out for liberty and death and for the hearts of a grieving nation. They explain why the homework isn't done, and why the relationship is. We hear them tumbling out of trembling lips and frozen in time on voice messages, and shouted to the balcony from the sidewalk below. His words set us laughing and crying and weeping and wailing; how different life would be with a man without words.

Confidentiality

His lips are sealed. You can tickle him and threaten him, but he just won't tell. He promised that he would keep it under his hat and that's where it will stay. They can throw him in jail and throw away the key, but he won't divulge his sources. You can beg and plead and cajole, but he still won't spill what he knows about the scandal in City Hall. He won't share even the tiniest tidbit about the deathbed conversation he had with his uncle, even though the man's been gone for thirty years. He doesn't believe in giving hints. He believes that changing names to protect the innocent still leaves him guilty as sin. Sorry, but his talk with Will was confidential, and anyway, it's not his job to be a spy for your best friend, who just happens to be Will's wife. Really, he was told in the strictest confidence, and yes, that means you, too. *How would you feel if I betrayed a confidence with you?* he asks. *Just between you and me, I'd be madder than a hornet, but that's different of course, don't you see?*

Laughter

Big, deep, belly laughs that bring tears to his eyes and leave him clutching his sides and pounding his foot on the floor. That one, particular laugh he laughs only when he watches Robin Williams and Billy Crystal at the same time. *Stop it guys, you're killing me!* Quiet laughter that barely makes its way out of his mouth and seems to wiggle out of his eyes instead. That tight, nervous laugh he laughed when the border patrol asked to see his passport and he knew he had left it back in the room. *Ha, ha, well sir, it's like this, ha, ha!* The knowing laugh shared between those who get the inside joke. The strained laugh of those who don't. *Well, I guess you had to be there!* Uncontrollable laughter when it just feels so darned good. *No, yes, No! You have to stop. Really, you have to!* His own rendition of the cartoon villain laugh. *Nyeh-eh-eh!* His Woody Woodpecker laugh. *(Your voice here!)* The laugh that makes him sound like a jackass. *Hee-haw! Hee-haw! Hee-haw!*

Eros

Cupid pulled back his bow and hit a bull's eye, and now the man is real, real gone. He's leaking love all over the place and sucking the deliciousness out of life. He's stopping to smell the roses and sticking around to taste the dripping flesh of a ripe and juicy mango. He sees lovers cavorting in the clouds and alongside the road and he's trembling with runaway lust. Suddenly, all is sensational! Birdsong sweeter than he's ever heard lilts across meadows more lush than he's ever seen. A light rain sprinkles his face and he rises up into rapture. He trades in flannel for silk, and cotton for satin, and finally chucks it all to run naked 'neath the moon. Love songs spill out of his lips without the slightest provocation, and he stays home from work on account of desire. He craves deep chocolate ice cream with hot raspberry syrup, passion fruit nectar with a twist, and Pavarotti twenty-four hours a day. He's washing in rosewater and soaking in ylang-ylang. He's been struck by an arrow, and he's taken it to heart.

Surprises

Surprise! He called to tell you he'd be home for the holidays, and ten minutes later showed up at the door. He said he was bringing someone home to dinner, and it turned out to be the sister you hadn't seen for seventeen years. *Surprise!* Pack your bag and be sure to grab your bathing suit; your tickets are waiting at the airport. Don't look now, but he shaved his head. Don't look again; but his nipple is pierced. It's his fiftieth birthday, and he doesn't know it yet, but his friends all chipped in for his vasectomy. On the spur of the moment, he quit his job and joined the circus. In the blink of an eye, he cashed in his bonds and bought a houseboat and he's setting sail for the islands. *Surprise!* While you were out, he finished his thesis and polished the kitchen floor. He also polished off the cakes that you made for the bake sale. He didn't know the real estate agent had stopped by, until she got to the bathroom. *Surprise!*

Conversation

conversation

Starting light and breezy, weather and sports and films. Then, without warning, you're trading your stories of love and loss. Recounting your combined total of sixty-three jobs. Sharing family histories and simultaneously getting lumps in your throats. Hearing about the summer he was a nanny for three spoiled kids on the West side of town. Dissecting American civilization and the national social fabric and how it's all going to hell in a hand basket. Topic: Who could *ever* replace Seinfeld? Who could *ever* replace Johnny Carson? What you imagine you would do if imprisoned in a concentration camp. Followed promptly by what members of your family did when they were. How much everyone misses John Lennon. Why he never wants to be a father. Why he wants to be one, more than anything. The meaning of life. The gender of God. Your fears of death. Why the idea of photosynthesis is so cool. Your blistering commentary on big-money-elections; his impassioned support for the plight of Tibet. How quickly time passes when you talk with a man.

Humility

A humble man isn't lowly; he just lives close to the earth. He bows and scrapes to no other man; he simply pulls himself down from the heights of pride and pretension, and lives a life free of arrogance. A humble man is rooted in modesty. A humble man assumes nothing. When the spotlight shines on him, he quietly steps aside. When credit is tossed in his direction, he passes it to his teammates, his employees, his co-workers, his God. When he is asked to say a few words, he says a very few. When others call him a hero, he simply states that he's a human being, doing what humans do. If singled out for salvos, he shrugs and says *Hey, just doing my job*. No matter how well others may think of him, he prefers to think well of others. When a man tells you just how humble he is, it's safe to assume that he's not.

Truth
truth

There's a lot more to the truth than just facts. Or consequences. Truth be told, it matters little whether a man *tells* the truth, unless he also *lives* it. Unless he lives the truth, the whole truth, and nothing but the truth of his life. The genuine article; the very life he was born to live. It is one thing to stand in a court of law and swear to be truthful; it is something else altogether to stand in front of the mirror and commit to live a life without lies. When a man creates a life in tune with his deepest knowings, he lives in his truth. When a man forsakes the agendas of others and lives according to his highest values, he can truthfully say he is living an authentic life. The truth is sometimes bitter, and often strange. To get to the naked truth of his own existence, a man may have to peel away lifetimes of layers of lies. When he does, he will find his truth, his way, and his life.

Vision

O say, can you see the vast horizon of a man's vision? Where others see a house, he sees a community and a gentler way for people to inhabit the Earth. Where others see a recycling center, his crystal ball shows an entire new industry fueled by friendly enzymes that gleefully chomp on our trash. He doesn't want just a website—he sees the next generation of e-commerce, socially responsible and technologically profound. Elect him, and he'll forge a new and improved democratic process. Loan him $10,000, and he'll create a global network of locally owned banks offering micro-credit to neighbors moving toward self-sufficiency. He's a teacher with big ideas on reforming education to tap new levels of human potential, and his perspectives on relationships and family can rock our world. Who cares if he can't find his glasses? With the kind of vision he's got, he can see forever.

Ins & Outs

ins & outs

He's in love, he's out of favor. He's out of the bedroom; he's back in the den. Count him in for the stock deal; but if it starts to slide, count him out. He's in the money! He's in the poorhouse. He's in the pink! He's out of gas. He's sitting in a corner office with a view of the city, and suddenly he's out on the street with six months of severance. He's in the flow; he's out of sync. He's reached the inner sanctum, but he's out of the loop. He got himself into a serious jam and nobody's getting him out of this one except you-know-who. He used to stand in the shadows, and now he's an out-and-out standout. He was in his best season ever, and then he struck out, and now he's in retirement. He's in great health and he's out of chemo. He's out of debt and he's into simplicity. Out of rehab and back in the groove. Out of his clothes and into the hot tub. He's in way too deep; he's out of his league; he's out on the edge and he loves it!

Smile

Oh, that smile! That shy, boyish grin slipping out of that slightly crooked mouth, waking up dimples and landing on everyone within smiling distance. That brilliant, white smile you can thank the orthodontist for. That toothless smile that still illuminates the room after all these years. The broad, slightly sad smile you've seen on every male in every family photo. The smile that flashes *I love you* without a word. The double-wide smile that filled his face when he met his twins for the first time. The shaky smile he smiles to hide the tears, and the sheepish smile he smiles when he realizes he's hiding nothing at all. Can you imagine that smile of all smiles that no one else has ever seen? *Say Cheese!* Today you are a man! *Say Cheese!* You passed the exam! *Say Cheese!* You're on the summit! *Say Cheese!* You light up the world when you smile!

Competence

It's a pleasure to watch a man do what he knows how to do. To see him tie the perfect fly, compose a soul-stirring concerto, flawlessly complete a crossword puzzle with a fountain pen. What a privilege to see him hang the painting just right, finding the stud in the wall without endlessly banging about, and setting the nail at the perfect angle on the first try. What a joy it is when he braids his little girl's hair in cornrows and irons her favorite dress. *How come even his first waffle of the morning doesn't stick?* Somehow he knows just what kind of knot works where. Just which solvent softens the glue without stripping the varnish. Exactly how to read a sonnet, pausing and pondering with poetic precision. Like a pro, he sharpens knives and hangs wallpaper, mends a gaping hole in his hand-knit wool sweater, takes the creak out of the heirloom rocker, and knows what to say when the IRS calls. Even if there's only one thing he can do, we're delighted when he does it so well.

Defiance
defiance

Hell no, he won't go! And he defies anyone to try and stop him. He's one of the original defiant ones. He'll walk out of that hospital under his own power, and he doesn't care what the doctors or the insurance companies say. He'll defy all the odds to get his business off the ground and make it profitable by the end of Year One. He thinks your conditions stink, and he'd rather go it alone and you can take your trust fund and put it where the sun doesn't shine. He's not about to follow the crowd like lemmings off the side of a cliff. No way. No how. He'll never buckle under to their outrageous demands. If they want him, they'll have to take him kicking and screaming. He's a rebel with a cause. Put on your life jacket, because he's about to make waves and he's not interested in taking any prisoners. Go ahead, make his day. He dares you.

Roots

He's Cockney through and through, and damned proud of it! His mother was a slave in North Carolina, a wet-nurse who loved everybody's children as if they were her own. He comes from a long line of fortune-tellers, itinerants who showed up with music and magic and were chased out of every town they stopped in. Somebody, somehow related to someone, sailed from England on the Mayflower. His people have been in Colombia forever, and before he left, he knew every person in his village by name. The men before him were always tailors, and once dressed the family of the Emperor. For three generations before him, no one in his family had ever been off the reservation. He is the first-born son of the first-born son of a full-blooded African Queen. His family's apartment was always filled with intellectuals, Communists who pounded the table and drank steaming pots of coffee. His mother was a midwife, like her mother and her mother and her mother and hers. *You come from good peasant stock*, his grandmother always said. *And don't you ever forget it!*

Home

Be it ever so humble, a man's home is his castle. Or his yurt or his tepee or his room with a hot plate or his camper or his truck or his tent. He's got a futon on the floor and a signed Picasso on the wall. A settee he's never sat on, and an exercise bike that hasn't left the laundry room since he gave it up for Lent. His study is perfectly appointed with leather, with oak and with neo-Georgian style. Unread mail piles up on the counter, unwashed towels heap high in the hall. No fingerprints on his glass-topped table, no tracks on his Oriental rugs, no cartoons on his smudge-free fridge. He invites the squirrels in every other day to clean off his counters and lick up his floor. He vacuums thrice daily and shudders if people do not shuck their shoes. He's chosen to be master of his domain in a basement apartment. King of the hill in the handmade house of his dreams. Lord of the manor atop Nob Hill and solitary squatter out under the stars. It's home and it's his and it's warm and he's safe. And whenever he's there, he is home.

pillow talk

A man can lapse into loquaciousness just when the lights have gone out. You're ready to sleep, and he wants to know how many left-handed people are on the planet. Give or take twenty million. Suddenly, he needs to understand the details of the new farm support legislation. He's pondering his final resting place and considering the pros and cons of cremation. You're dancing off to dreamland, and he wants to talk sustainable land use. After thirty-five years of sleeping together, he's noticing that your nose is crooked and he wants to talk about it now. The room is dark and the night is still, and he's remembering the summer of '71. He's waxing poetic about the ultimate burrito he had at lunch. Which reminds him of the time he hitchhiked through Baja, California. Which reminds him of the Beach Boys music, the lyrics of which he begins to sing. You love these quiet moments so. The quiet voices, softened tones. But you're ready to sleep and you ask him gently *Will you please put your head in your pillow?*

Magnetism

There you are, minding your own business, when suddenly and without warning, you are drawn to a man like a moth to a flame. It makes no sense. It's not what he looks like or what he's wearing or what he's doing. He may be standing at a buffet table trying to balance a plateful of chicken wings, or tossing egg cartons into a dumpster at the recycle center. The only thing remarkable about him might be his ordinariness. And, of course, that indefinable magnetism. Nothing in your rational mind can explain the attraction. One moment you don't even notice he's there, and the next, you are caught in a powerful force field that pulls you in and holds you like a cartoon clipping plastered to the refrigerator door. You turn away, only to find your focus pulled back in his direction. The next thing you know, you're making plans for dinner and a movie, and filing your income tax together. Like filings held fast by a magnet.

kisses

Inside a man's mouth are a multitude of kisses. Sweet kisses, placed lightly on neck napes and behind ears and elegantly on the back of a lady's hand. Oh-so-tender, tiny kisses on the cheek of a two-year-old, on the wrinkled face of his dying grandmother. Long, hard, and searching kisses, peckish and oh-what-the-heckish kisses under the front porch light after the movies. Kisses planted on the earth, terra firma, beloved homeland where his great-grandfather died on a winter's eve. A single silent kiss on the top of the head, eyes open, eyes closed, kisses on toes and fingers and wherever else a man fancies. The kiss before, the kiss after. His very first kiss, his very last kiss, the kiss before the troops move out. Gentle and hesitating, all teeth and tongue and sweet nectar of the gods, a kiss is still a kiss when a man is ready to kiss.

Grit

grit

He's tough enough to take it. Would gargle with gravel if given the command. Has fallen out of more trees than a baby sparrow and tumbled down more hills than a pebble on a roll. Who knows how many bones he's broken? Been bucked by broncos and climbed back on for more. He mined coal long enough to know that it takes out of a man at least as much as it takes out of the earth. Worked fourteen-hour days in a mill and made it. He's had to do things with the butt of a rifle that he never thought anyone could. He works the homicide desk and the emergency room and holds it together when he has to. He works the fields from dawn to dusk, and barely stops for breathing. He's seen things no man ought to see, but he wouldn't turn away, so he saw them. He can bark like a bulldog and bite if he must. He can chew on boulders and reduce them to dust. He's as gentle as a lamb, but he's gritty to the core, and his grit is as true as all get-out.

Vests

We have a vested interest in a man who wears vests. Silky-backed, pleated, and belted, with a fob at the waist for pocket watch or a tucked-away, vest-pocket diary. Leather and suede or thick, curly sheepskin, naturally tanned or tooled and dyed. Rainbow-hued and woven the old-fashioned way, worn all the way home from his trip to Peru. Down vests that keep him warm, and fleece vests that keep him moving all winter. Vests over shirts and undershirts and with nothing under them at all. *Buttoned, unbuttoned, open and flapping, vests on bare chests may incite cheers and clapping.* Aren't vests of the West truly the best? Perfect for poker and bankers and stagecoach drivers, and bar-keeps in dusty old last-chance saloons. When it comes to a three-piece suit, give us the vest—you can just chuck the rest. With the power invested in him, he's perfectly dressed. Even though he's not wearing a stitch save his vest.

Treasures

He keeps them in cedar-scented boxes or bubble-pak envelopes or displayed where he can enjoy them every day. Sometimes they're in his car, hanging from the rear-view mirror, or next to the seat, where he can touch them anytime. The tiny note that was taped to the bathroom mirror the day he left. The shells he picked up at his favorite lagoon. The stones shaped like hearts that he finds whenever he takes the time to look. The military medal his Dad gave him when he was nine. Dried petals from the one time someone sent him roses. The glass vial of dirt from the family land. Meemaw's favorite china teacup, with the chip in the rim. The stale half-bar of chocolate they promised to save until next time. Pesos from Mexico, his lucky token from the Reno truck stop, the garnet that someone pressed into his hand moments before the crash. Pictures of everything that was perfect before it soured. Pictures of what's perfect now. Rings returned and watches wound down. Collections collecting dust and trinkets turned to treasures.

Heart
heart

Oh! To feel the beating of a man's heart! To trace the rutted pathways and hardened ridges, only to sink in as the edges soften. A man's heart is as big as all outdoors and twice as grand. It is a wilderness, often uncharted and shrouded in a mist of fear. Fear of a heart being broken, fear of the aching heart. A man's heart is his seat of love; filled with compassion for others and for himself. It bursts to overflowing at the sight of his child, at the mere mention of his beloved, or at the thought of his God. And, like any muscle, the heart is strengthened when used often and challenged well. It does a man's heart good to give of himself from the bottom of his heart. To fall in love with life and love to his heart's content. He may wear his heart on his sleeve, dripping a bleeding trail behind him. He may approach us with his heart in his mouth and unable to speak the words of the heart. Take heart and know that all is not lost: The way to a man's heart is straight through your own.

WYSIWYG

wysiwyg

With some men, *What You See Is What You Get*. It's not that he's simple, it's that he's delightfully uncomplicated. He lives in a flesh-and-blood world and not in a sea of illusion and hyperbole. He enjoys a natural humility and has no truck with grandiosity. He works hard at what he does, and his goals will stretch him in many ways, yet will not pull him to the breaking point. He recognizes something larger than himself, and makes space for It in his life. He is honest with himself and others, and wears no masks of deceit or treachery. Chances are he will tell you about his weaknesses before you ever see them in action. He is generous to a fault, and is not prone to self-absorption and narcissism. If his life has afforded him some measure of privilege, he is grateful yet not flaunty. Know that you will not wake up one day to find this man has suddenly become something altogether different. There are no disclaimers around his neck: *What You See Is What You Get*.

kindness

He's the kind of man who fills his days with small acts of kindness. You know the kind. Kind of neighborly, shoveling snow for the shut-ins just in case today's the day they decide to go out. Kind of big-hearted, offering to carry the groceries for a young mother struggling with a double-wide stroller and a babe in arms. Kind of gentle, kneeling to comfort the cat with the fresh cut in his tail. He's the one who stopped by with a check after he heard that Jim passed over without even leaving enough behind to buy a casket. The one who scoured the mall for hours, trying to locate the owner of the wallet he found. He's the one who gave the homeless man a job, when so many others wouldn't give him the time of day. He always has a warm smile for a stranger, and a kind word, and a sympathetic ear. He's just that kind of man. You know the kind.

Composure

He stood in front of seven microphones and thirty photographers, and amid all the whirring and clicking, he never even flinched. He sat through a two-hour interview for the biggest job of his life, and he hardly even blinked. When the decision came down and the others were anxious, he handled it all with aplomb. He was cool and collected the day of the bombing, and he was confident he knew what to do. He faced a hostile audience and the lights went out, and he never lost a single line. When he bathed his baby for the very first time, he knew that he never would drop her. It was the last round of the tournament and he had one frame to go, and his hands were as steady as granite. He was confident he would get the loan; he was certain his testimony would make the difference; he never doubted that right would win out. When the winners were named, he was the picture of poise, an unqualified pro at composure.

Silence
silence

Don't be fooled into thinking he's not there when he is not talking. He's speaking volumes if you can listen to the sound of silence. Just try. Follow him into the stillness and hear the words he does not say. Feel the quality of his silence and enter into it with ease. What blessed relief are the white spaces on a page of printing! How sweet the silences that punctuate a symphony! A pregnant pause is ripe with revelation! Let go of your fear that a lack of words means a lack of feeling. Or that an empty mouth reflects an empty heart. Remember, still waters run deep. Remember, the way to navigate the forest with grace and speed, is to concentrate on the spaces between the trees instead of the trees themselves. Let yourself navigate his silence instead of bumping into his words.

Personality

personality

It doesn't matter what kind it is, as long as he's got some. He can be bashful and bookish and barely audible as he whispers in the library reference stacks—and he'll captivate with his love of the literate. He can duel on the deck of a pirate ship with swashbuckling derring-do, engaging in death-defying sword play in a show of élan. A man can rock his world simply by being; with a quiet presence that's unmistakably his. He can be the one who's always heard above the crowd, or the one who's nearly silent. One man builds empires that last for eons; another builds castles that sink in the sand. He may study art history or make history or make personal statements from art made with glass. Rugged or refined or refreshingly neither, he can be a lover or a fighter or a little of both. When his masks are removed and you meet him in person, you can be certain a man's personality is his.

Polish
polish

He's as smooth as well-oiled mahogany! He's lacquered and lustred and all lotioned up, and not a smidgen of schmutz on his collar. His small talk is as brilliant as the shine on his shoes, and his manner is gently genteel. He knows who to call and, for him, they will answer. He knows how to beckon so, yes, they will call. His pedigree is pages long, and he's got the pedicure to prove it. He's all spit and polish, with none of the spit. He can always can get a corner table, even when the restaurant's been booked up for months. He orders in French when he's dining in Paris, and he's confidently sure of which fork he should pluck. He can suavely slurp through a plate of spaghetti, and not one strand will slip onto his shirt. While others clamor for attention, he quietly commands it. He's never affected; it's part of his breeding. He's as permanently polished as a never-wax floor.

Feelings

He's angry over the incident in the alley. He's frightened by the way he feels, and he's afraid he's going to blow it. He's deliriously happy, and he just can't hide it. *He's so excited!* He's never felt so embarrassed in his life, and it shows all over his face. He was so enraged that he said those awful words—and now he feels sad that he said them. *He feels so frustrated—and he can't do a thing!* He feels overwhelmed and he's lost his perspective. He feels guilty for what happened, and no matter what you say, he's still going to feel guilty feelings. He feels incredibly stupid and he feels like he's about six years old. It all feels so good and so pure, it can only be bliss, and he's feeling the joy rise inside him. He feels like crying. He feels like flying. He feels like dancing around the room with glee, so he does. He feels numb, feels empty. He can't feel a thing and he knows it, and that's the worst feeling of all.

Eyes
eyes

Why do bedroom eyes get all the glory? What about hungry and thirsty kitchen eyes? Moist and steamy bathroom eyes? Eyes all but hidden with a sweep of long lashes, or magnified by glasses sliding down his nose. Winking eyes, blinking eyes, *Oh my God I'm sinking* eyes! Sky-blue eyes, Hi you!-eyes, Try-me, Fly-me, Why-me? eyes. Eyes that pull you into a vortex of his soul. Sad and sorry eyes, dripping with apology and asking forgiveness. Dark and deep and brooding eyes that signal *Stay away*; scared eyes you look at but they never look back. Eyes that meet across a crowded room, dancing a pas de deux of *Who's watching whom?* The eyes so familiar the very first time you saw them, greenish-gray and flecked with gold. Your grandfather's kind and knowing eyes, sparkling bright behind lush, unkempt brows, and dull and vacant as he slipped away. *Don't look now, but he's watching you!* It's written all over his eyes.

Mischief
mischief

A terminal troublemaker at two and a hell-raising hooligan at fifteen. Thank goodness he's still a rabble-rouser today! He knows exactly who disabled the spark plugs on the bulldozer the day the old church was slated to come down (*and even though he's got grease on his hands, he isn't about to come clean*). You can bet he knows something about the pounds of putrid pork fat that were delivered COD to his Senator in Washington (*but then again, who can say?*) He's got more than a pinch of naughty to balance out his nice. Dennis the Menace has been his hero ever since Mr. Wilson's petunias mysteriously found their way into Margaret's panty drawer. Can he help it if his elbow accidentally flipped the main circuit while he walked through corporate headquarters the day of the big layoff? He's a little bit Luddite with a devilish dash, and some would call him a rascal. He may misbehave, *but he's misunderstood*, and he's proud to be called Mr. Mischief.

Sorrows

His father left for the war just after he was born, and never came back. His mother was an artist who never had the freedom to paint, and once she left home, there was nothing he could do to help her. He was young and scared, and he didn't stick around long enough to meet his first-born child. He betrayed the one he loved most, for the favors of one he never loved at all. He turned away from his shadows, and never sought to bring them into the light of day. Not once did he allow himself to surrender to anything vast and omnipotent. He did everything he thought he was supposed to do, and in the end, he made everybody happy but himself. He sat on the fence for far too long, until the choice was no longer his to make. He never made the time to show how much he cared. He tried his darnedest to give, yet forgot to ask what they wanted to receive. He desperately wanted help, but pride got in his way. He thought it could wait until later, but later never came.

Perfection
perfection

When it comes to perfection, he's a paragon. Every hair in his nose is perfectly groomed; all his teeth are in perfect alignment. His linen suit is perfectly wrinkled and his shoes have been perfectly polished. He has the perfect art collection, perfectly hung on perfectly painted walls. To hear him tell it, he has the perfect job, the perfect lover, the perfect home, and the perfect life. Without a doubt, he's a perfect bore. If someone puts the wrong spoon in the wrong position, he goes perfectly wild. A faux pas can send him into perfect paroxysms. A perfectionist? *Puh-leeze.* Discriminating? *Definitely.* Anal? *Absolutely.* His Saturday salons are sheer perfection, and he has the clippings to prove it. His pedigreed poodles are perfectly sublime. He's finicky to a fault. *And his friends are all flawless!* When his pursuit of perfection makes him perfectly obnoxious, we love his imperfect perfection.

Conflicts

How can I show you who I really am, when I don't even know myself? How can I share with you my vulnerable side, when everybody told me I had to be strong? What if I want to spend the rest of my life with a man? What if I want to spend the rest of my life with a woman? How can it be that I've trashed my marriage vows all in the name of love? Who's going to teach my son how to love, when his father can hardly figure it out for himself? How can I become my own man, when my job and my church and my country always said I belonged to them? How do I stand in my personal power without stepping on other people's toes? How can I let go and not lose everything I've worked my whole life to get? How am I supposed to listen to that still, small voice inside, when the rooftop chatter in my head just gets louder all the time? What if I change, really change, and you don't like who I am? How do I follow my bliss and still pay the bills? How much longer can I keep doing the same things in the same way and expect anything to turn out differently?

Romance
romance

At the heart of romance, there lies man. Lounging in the grass, gazing at the stars. Lying on a bearskin rug, in front of a raging fire. He's on a flight of fancy and flowers fill the air. He's riding a white SUV through a gentle rain, and stopping at the mall to buy beeswax candles. *Romeo, Romeo, wherefore art thou?* He's turning down the lighting and turning on Bocelli, and turning up the heat in more ways than one. He's splashing a dash of citrus in the most unlikely places. The romantic man of the millennium serenades with your favorite CD. He's proposing marriage on the billboard at the traffic circle. Look! Up in the sky! He's writing your name right next to a cloud! He packs a perfect picnic, and he won't forget the paté. Your voice mail's on overload, and all of it rhymes. Time once was, when a man was romantic. Aren't we delighted that now is that time?

Details

A man is in the details. The way he wears his hat. The way he still wears that battered, old fraternity ring, every day without fail. His CDs, indexed by last name, country of origin, and first letter of the first word of the first line. His kitchen spices, grouped by color and labeled in eight-point type, never nine. The eleven volumes of recorded dreams, starting with the first one he remembered as a child, that whale dream, every one dated and cross-referenced according to key themes and symbols. His perfectly clean-shaven face (*How does he do that without a mirror?*), perfectly pressed dress shirts, glasses with nary a smudge, the always-fresh flower in the tiny vase on the dash of his car. The way he makes the bed so there's not one wrinkle on one sheet. That cleaning-the-sink-thing with the sponges left lying equidistant from the counter edges, facing true north. His signature, with a circle over the *i* and never a dot. What perfection we find in a man's detailia!

Chaos
chaos

On the way to order, a man's bound to run into more than a little chaos. He'll start having pork rinds with his tofu, and he'll listen to Zappa while he's being Zen. He'll leave his lover and quit his job and won't touch the laundry for weeks. He'll grow out his sideburns and start growing anise in the attic, and he'll breed baby rats where his laptop once lived. Everything will turn upside down and inside out, and let's not even mention the kitchen. He'll get all his stuff out of storage and leave it strewn around the living room, boxes half empty and crates to be opened and *what's that* and *whatnot* piled high and waist-deep. He'll say *Yes* and then he'll say *No*, and before the week is out, he'll consider *Yes* again. He's moving north, but he doesn't know why, and he's not even sure how to get there. It might smell kind of funky like something fermenting—and in the midst of the chaos, it is.

old-world charm

He may be third-generation Cincinnati, but he charms us with his old-world ways. Something in him reflects a different time and different place, where everything moves more slowly and his watch is always set for the here and now. You'll find him sitting at an outdoor cafe, reading yesterday's paper and savoring espresso or a baguette with jam. He's delighted to see the meter maid, since he rode his trusty, one-speed bike and left it safely unlocked. He's wearing a sports coat, a vest, and a hat, and his shoes are more suited for strolls on the boulevard than for sprinting a lunchtime 5K. He carries his coins in a most charming change purse, and his bills he keeps tucked in a flap on his belt. Saturday mornings, promptly at nine, he walks to the barber shop for a shave and a haircut, then stops by his neighbor's for a hot cup of tea. He's a frequent browser at second-hand bookstores; and his apartment is filled with old etchings and prints. His word processor is a pencil, and his network is BBC. When he greets us, we feel we've been properly greeted; when he nods in farewell, we feel charmed, to be sure.

bonds

These are the ties that bind. The incredible bond between mother and son, which remains long after the cord is cut and the apron strings unloosed. The bond that he forged with his father, however raw or imperfect it might have been; and with his own children, daughters and sons alike, linked for eternity. Men connect when they work together, when they play together, when they live together and shower together and, if they're lucky, cry together. He will always have a link to his first love, whether or not they ever lay eyes on each other again. He will never lose that indescribable bond that men share in war; that could never be understood by those of us who were not there. His deepest and strongest bonds may be created through shared love or pain, or struggle or triumph. The best bonds will never choke him, but will strengthen and encourage him, whether by blood or fate or intention.

Cooking

He's cooking with gas! He's firing up the grill! He's unwrapping last
night's pizza and eating it cold with mayonnaise! There's a duck
marinating in the fridge and homemade elderberry wine aging in the
cellar. He's whipping up a light supper for six, fried green tomatoes and
chess pie and an artichoke thing that's to die for. His Shiitake mush-
room and salmon soup is simmering as we speak. It's a seven-course
Chinese banquet, and he flew the tea in from Beijing. It's pasta again
for the twelfth day running, and this time he's topping it with tuna. He's
strolling through the farmer's market finding the perfect fennel. Doing
something unforgettable with olive oil. Building a fire out back to boil
the lobsters. Home on the range, he's cleaning out the refrigerator and
cooking up a mess of something or other in a cast-iron skillet. With
cheese, the man is a whiz! We're starving, we're famished, we're faint-
ing with hunger! We'll ravish a man when he's cooking!

lips

How lovely, how luscious, his lips! Pressed up against the icy window and leaving a chilly first impression. Gently grazing cheeks at the high school reunion. Thin and elegant lips nearly hidden between mustache and beard and making a rare opening night appearance. Thick, thicker, the thickest, most succulent lips rosy and rich and ripe and red. Lips smeared with butterscotch pudding, with melting pistachio ice cream, with lipstick of a shade clearly not his own. Lips swollen from all-night, every-night jam sessions. *Don't get lippy with me!* his mother scolded, when she asked *Whose lips are those on your collar?* Lips as moist as summer dew, sweetened and softened with cocoa butter. Lips split from splitting logs under the desert sun; and chapped from riding into an arctic wind. Lip-smacking, chip-snacking lips. Salty lips, spicy lips, lips-you've-nearly-eaten lips. Lips bitten and buttoned from holding back; upper lips stiffened from years of biting the bullet when he'd rather kiss the sky. Here's a lip tip: If he says *Read my lips*, ask for the version in Braille.

Spirit

spirit

It is something so sacred, this spirit of a man. We can neither touch it nor see it, nor hold it in our hands. When we are lucky, we may catch a whiff of it as it slips out through unguarded gateways. We will at once feel its presence. It may be unfamiliar, yet we will recognize it as hearty and earthy and essentially male. We will taste his ache in the air. The spirit of a man wants so much to be free! To run without shoes and navigate without a compass and live the life men were born to live. It is something so vital, this spirit of a man. It carries with it a light that can show a man a way through the darkness. It will enliven his work and invigorate his play, and string a golden strand that connects with his soul. A spirited man is a man born of spirit: He's unlimited in nature and eternally free.

Je ne sais quoi

je ne sais quoi

There's a quality about a man that's so *I don't know what*. I mean to say, it's nearly impossible to put your finger on it. I know you know what I'm talking about. It's what makes him so delightfully this. And so delectably that. Who can put it into words? When you think you've got it down, the whole thing flies up in your face again. Can you appreciate that? I know that you can. It's just that a man possesses a whole lot of what can only be described as *I don't know what*. I can't put it any more clearly than that. It's like describing why the Internet works. It's like trying to teach someone how to breathe. I know you get what I'm saying. This thing that we love about a man, it's all rather elusive. Maybe it's spiritual. Or biochemical. I know they've all got some; but *I don't know what*.

about the author

About the Author

Rachel Snyder is a mother, writer, performer, inspiratrix, and lover of men (not necessarily in that order). She is the author of *365 Words of Well-Being for Women*, and has written much more, most of which you've probably never seen but undoubtedly would enjoy a great deal. Rachel Snyder would love to speak to your group or event, and would love to hear from you. Write to P.O. Box 313, Boulder, CO 80306.